The Luminary of Indian Cinema

Parthajit Baruah

Ukiyoto Publishing

All global publishing rights are held by

Ukiyoto Publishing

Published in 2025

ISBN 9789371822572

www.ukiyoto.com

Dedication

I would like to dedicate this book to the two stalwarts of Manipuri cinema:

M.K. Binodini and G. Narayan Sharma.

Foreword

There is something peculiar about writing the foreword to one's own biography. But I am doing it here, all the same, considering two things. I intend it as an appreciation of Parthajit Baruah's work. I understand that this work is a part of a larger project, which started with a well-received and discussed biography on Adoor Gopalakrishnan. Gopalakrishnan sets a precedent for me by writing the Preface.

Parthajit's work here is much more than the subject i.e., me. It tells the story of a shared condition of making films against all odds in our region. The odds are still there, but alternative technologies and forums have made the situation a bit better. Getting our voices heard, though, still remains challenging. Our voice is not loud, for we are much fewer in number, and it tends to get drowned amongst already established voices on an already set agenda. This aspect of my experience finds a place in Parthajit's argument that my films are acts of resistance.

Language is at the core of expressions. Diverse languages set grounds for a diversity of expressions. Without a theoretical apparatus, it seems to me now, I had intuitively tried to enrich the language(s), both linguistic and otherwise, that was bestowed upon me. I am glad that Parthajit has perceived this strand and delineates the cultural and historical background of my works.

We reach out to those who speak other languages, in the conviction that languages are inter-translatable. I listened to what my tradition wishes to teach me, and imbibed its sensibilities. I listened to the great masters from other lands with open ears. And in the process, something came out that I claimed as mine.

At one point, I decided not to make films funded by private producers. The reasons for that decision are documented in this book. The decision inevitably led to applying for funds from public agencies. Prospects of funding need so called tangible "recognition" and "achievements". Recognition, thus, served as a means of making more films. If recognition helps to create more films, then I welcome it. The matter, more or less, ends there. What ultimately matters, upon reflection at this ripe age, is that my works have given inspiration and strength to filmmakers from our region. I appreciate Parthajit for his conversations with filmmakers and artists from the north-east.

It is my good fortune that I have been able to make films for such a long span of time. I have had a long run as an artist. Age has made the run slower, but I intend to continue it, some more.

Aribam Syam Sharma

Imphal, Manipur, July, 2025

Preface

A book detailing the life, times and achievements of the renowned Manipuri filmmaker, Aribam Syam Sharma should have been written long ago, preferably when he was in his prime. Young Parthajit Baruah has done with enviable success what someone from our generation should have done.

Parthajit shows remarkable powers of observation, analysis and judgment as he goes about letting us into the quiet, meditative world of one of India's foremost filmmakers. That Aribam Syam Sharma is not as widely known or deeply appreciated outside the North-East as he doubtless deserves to be is a matter of more sadness than shame. Ironically, at least two of his best films are still the toast of many a cultural capital in the West.

I hope this well-argued and well-stated book will go at least some way in making film-lovers living in the plains aware of the lasting truth and beauty of Syam Sharma's oeuvre. I feel honoured to have written the preface to an important book on an extraordinary artist inching towards his 90th year.

Parthajit is that rare film person who writes on films, but also makes films himself. Previously, he has done a handsome book on Adoor Gopalakrishnan, which has come for praise in well-defined circles. Understandably, Parthajit's primary area of interest is the North-East, but this has not prevented him from spreading his wings farther. Needless to emphasize, such an attitude at a time when dark winds are blowing across the land, deserves all the support we can muster.

Vidyarthy Chatterjee
August, 2025
Kolkata

Prologue

My first meeting with Aribam Syam Sharma began at the "Film, North-East, 2016" seminar in Itanagar, Arunachal Pradesh, from February 17 to 20, 2016. The seminar was part of a film festival organized by the Information and Public Relations department and the Film Federation of Arunachal. The primary focus of the seminar was to address the specific difficulties faced by filmmakers from the North-Eastern region of India when working in other parts of the country, often referred to as Mainland India. A diverse panel of filmmakers from the North-East shared their insights, including Kivini Shohe from Nagaland, Tribeny Rai from Sikkim, Napo RZ Thanga from Mizoram, Meena Longjam from Manipur, and the author of this book. The session was presided over by Aribam Syam Sharma, a highly respected and experienced filmmaker, who also shared his own experiences and the obstacles he had faced throughout his career. I was deeply moved by the way he described the challenges and successes of filmmakers from the North-East. I found myself fascinated and followed him during the festival, recording his lectures. Over time, I continued to meet him in various places, including Guwahati, Itanagar and his home city, Imphal, often accompanied by two young filmmakers, Monjul Baruah and Khanjan

Kishore Nath, who helped me in recording our discussions on video.

In this book, I have chosen to refer to the filmmaker as "Pabung Aribam" instead of "Syam Sharma" or "Sharma." I believe the use of "Pabung Aribam" offers a stronger connection to the Manipuri cultural context. In the Meitei community of Manipur, "Pabung" means both biological father and a paternal figure, representing someone knowledgeable and influential of similar age to one's father, reflecting the culture's deep-rooted customs. Moreover, I have avoided referring to him as "Aribam Sir" for the sake of readability in this book. Just as "Adoor," a place in Kerala, symbolizes the cinematic greatness of Adoor Gopalakrishnan, so too does "Pabung Aribam" represent the distinct style and enduring impact of Aribam Syam Sharma on Indian cinema.

I would like to mention two contemporary filmmakers who, like Aribam Syam Sharma, have deeply influenced my understanding and appreciation of film: the late Shyam Benegal and Adoor Gopalakrishnan. My engagement with their works has been so deep that I felt urge to write books on their journey. I'm now writing Shyam Benegal's film legacy, a project I'm actively working on. In 2016, I completed my book, *Face to Face: The Cinema of Adoor Gopalakrishnan*, which explores Adoor's unique narrative style and the thematic concerns of his films. Both Benegal and Adoor have been bestowed with the prestigious Dada Saheb Phalke Award for their contributions to Indian cinema.

While exploring Benegal and Adoor's films, I am also intrigued by the unique perspective of Aribam Syam Sharma, an 89-year-old filmmaker and thinker from Manipur, whose experiences offer a different narrative. Pabung Aribam's films resonate celebrate the rich culture, traditions, and stories of Manipur, a region often neglected in the broader narratives of Indian cinema. While Benegal works with an extensive range of subjects, weaving social reforms, historical events, and human experiences into his films, and Adoor captures the nuances of Kerala's socio-political structure through his films, Pabung Aribam remains focused on the specific cultural narratives of Manipur.

Unlike Pabung Aribam, who faced unique challenges in Manipur, Benegal and Adoor worked in more secure and supportive filmmaking settings. On the other hand, Pabung's experiences in Manipur reflect the influence of local environment on a filmmaker's vision. His films express the beauty and diversity of Manipuri culture, moving beyond the common narrative of conflict. The disruptions in everyday life, with shops shuttered and streets deserted due to social unrest, present a stark contrast to the vibrant culture that Pabung strives to represent through his films. Many may overlook the significance of his commitment to showing Manipuri traditions and stories against such a backdrop of conflict. He wants the world to see that this region is not just a "disturbed zone" or defined solely by the "bandh culture". Instead, it is land rich in history, art, and tradition, he untiringly shows through his cinematic vision.

While Benegal, renowned for his impact on Indian parallel cinema, worked in an era marked by social and political transformation in India, a time that nonetheless allowed for artistic expression. His films frequently addressed social and political issues, yet the prevailing stability allowed him to concentrate more on the narrative itself. Similarly, Adoor, whose films deal with the politics, culture, and society of Kerala, made films in a conducive atmosphere.

Pabung's films frequently portray the essence of local struggles and cultural richness, even in the face of challenges. In contrast, the films of Benegal and Adoor, although addressing social and political issues, emerged from a context that allowed for greater experimentation with form and style, free from the relentless pressure of political turmoil. The differences among Pabung Aribam, Benegal, and Gopalakrishnan show the significance of a filmmaker's environment. Pabung Aribam's ability to establish the conditions for filmmaking in a challenging environment proves how constraints can inspire originality, whereas Benegal and Adoor's more advantageous circumstances show how an affirming setting can enable even deeper artistic exploration.

Pabung Aribam's body of work includes fifteen feature films and thirty-one non-feature films, along with his contributions as a music composer for twenty-five films. He won a remarkable fifteen national awards, six for feature films and nine for non-features besides winning multiple international awards. Film scholar Raghavendra (2009) states that Aribam Syam Sharma's career perhaps gives us the most compelling evidence of the insurmountable difficulties encountered by original talents in India when they set out to actually realise their dreams as filmmakers despite the presence of a state-run institution like the NFDC.

Consider his remarkable films, such as *Imagi Ningthem* (1981), which was awarded the Grand Prix at the Nantes Film Festival, and *Ishanou* (1990), which featured in the esteemed Un Certain Regard section at the Cannes Film Festival. Despite receiving international acclaim, the National Awards in India denied these films the recognition they deserved. These films, instead of winning the Golden Lotus (Swarna Kamal), received the Silver Lotus for Best Regional Film. It distinctly illustrates a systemic bias that frequently disregards the contributions of filmmakers from marginalised backgrounds. The awards run the risk of alienating a substantial portion of the audience that is in tune with these stories by neglecting to recognise the diversity and richness of regional cinema.

His experiences resonate deeply with the challenges many filmmakers from Northeast India face. During a press meet, he lamented, saying, "I faced the step motherly treatment in the film festivals several times. For instance, at the Indian panorama, Shekhar Kapoor was given more time to speak before the press at the International Film Festival of India, while I, along with Jahnu Barua and Dr. Bhabendra Nath Saikia, was clubbed together and given significantly less time. Eventually we had to walk away from the conference." These words reflect broader issues of recognition and representation within the Indian film industry. It clearly shows the marginalization faced by filmmakers from regions of North-East.

The book *Aribam Syam Sharma: The Luminary of Indian Cinema* comprises seven chapters, a prologue, and an introduction. The introduction, titled *The Unsung Maestro*, examines the viewpoints of filmmakers and critics from the Northeast, as well as those of Joshy Joseph, regarding the marginalisation of Pabung Aribam in national narratives. Chapter One, *Cinema of Manipur: A Symphony of Struggle and Hope*, explores the evolution of Manipuri cinema, providing readers with its cinematic and socio-political context. Chapter. Two, *From Dreams to Reality: The Aribam Saga Begins*, traces Pabung Aribam's journey from his childhood to his career as a filmmaker. Chapter Three, *1970s: Aribam's Iconic 3*, examines Pabung's three commercially successful films: *Lamja Parshuram* (1974), *Saaphabee* (1976), and *Olangthagee Wangmadasoo* (Even Beyond the Summer Horizon, 1980). Chapter Four, *Two Films, One Legacy*, shows how his landmark films, *Imagi Ningthem* (My Son,

My Precious, 1981) and *Ishanou* (The Chosen One, 1990), have established Manipuri cinema on the global stage. Chapter Five, *Voice from Shadows*, explores his lesser-known films and their impact on Manipuri cinema. Chapter Six, *Narrative Aesthetics: The Beauty of Visual Storytelling*, analyses his narrative and cinematic techniques. In Chapter Seven, titled *The Political Heart Behind the Lens*, the chapter examines the Pabung's body of work, which addresses various political issues. Through a close analysis of these films, it shows how Pabung subtly engages with socio-political contexts. Pabung adeptly combines personal narratives with broader societal commentary. The epilogue discusses his role in theatre and music. The book also includes an interview titled *In Conversation with Aribam Syam Sharma*, which offers insights into his core concepts. This book includes both film stills and working stills.

This book is my humble tribute to the significant contribution of Aribam Syam Sharma to Indian and Manipuri cinema. It addresses the challenges often faced by filmmakers from marginalized regions of the North-East. By focusing on Pabung Aribam's journey as a filmmaker, I hope readers will re-read his films and develop a deeper appreciation for the vital role of regional storytelling within Indian cinema.

Work Cited

Raghavendra, M.K. (2009). 50 INDIAN FILM CLASSICS. HarperCollins.

Contents

Introduction

The Unsung Maestro

Pabung Aribam is a distinguished filmmaker from Manipur, whose contributions have significantly shaped the landscape of Indian cinema, particularly within Manipuri cinema. His body of work has not only transformed the film scenario in Manipur but has also helped as a source of inspiration for emerging filmmakers in the North-East region. Growing up amidst rich cultural traditions, breath-taking landscapes, and vibrant stories, Pabung's personal experiences have profoundly influenced his filmmaking style. He possesses a unique skill to intricately weave the beauty of Manipuri culture and its deeply rooted stories into his cinematic works.

Pabung's contributions to Indian cinema, particularly in the context of Manipuri cinema, are substantial and worthy of greater recognition. Pabung is the first filmmaker from the North-East to win international award for *Imagi Ningthem* (My Son, My Precious, 1981). Pabung is the only Indian filmmaker to have won National Awards in both the Feature and Non-Feature Film categories in the same year, an extraordinary achievement he accomplished three timcs. These include *Ishanou* (1990) and *Indigenous Games of Manipur* (1990) at the 38th National Film Awards; *Sanabi* and *Yelhou Jagoi* (1995) at the 43rd National Film Awards; and *Leipaklei* and *Manipuri Pony*

(2012) at the 60th National Film Awards. His landmark works, such as *Imagi Ningthem* (My Son, My Precious, 1981) and *Ishanou* (The Chosen One, 1990), are not merely artistic pieces of work; they are explorations of the human condition that reflect deeply with both local and global audiences. One of the most distinctive aspects of Pabung's films is their lyrical and poetic tone. This attribute captivates audiences, evoking strong emotional responses. With his striking visual imagery, Pabung designs a unique cinematic experience that lingers long after the credits have rolled. His narrative flows naturally from one scene to the next, like a poem. Whether depicting the verdant landscapes of Manipur or capturing intimate moments between characters, his films reflect a deeper emotional level.

Nonetheless, despite their philosophical depth, these films frequently go unrecognised by mainstream Indian cinema, which typically favours more commercially feasible themes, as seen in Bollywood. This disparity shows the broader issue of cultural representation within Indian cinema, where regional voices often struggle for visibility. The Pickle quotes veteran filmmaker Adoor Gopalakrishnan, who spoke at the Bharati Niti-SIFCCI seminar on the Indian Entertainment Industry: Global Leader in Making. He stated, "There is a tendency to call any film made in a language other than Hindi as a regional film. We assert the fact that Indian cinema is made in several languages, and it is not limited to Bollywood. This is a very wrong term used because there is no such thing as a 'national film' in India. In the absence of a national film in the country, we cannot call any film as regional; we all together make the national film." Moreover, Adoor added, "It is high time we asserted that Indian cinema is made in several languages. To begin with, there are 14 national languages recognized by the Constitution, along with a few more" (The Pickle, 2018).

During the inauguration of the ninth edition of the Asian Film Festival at the National Film Archive of India (NFAI) on December 25, 2018, acclaimed filmmaker Jahnu Barua stated that Indians must accord more respect to regional cinema if films across various Indian languages are to gain an identity (*The Times of India*, 2018).

Distinguished filmmaker Girish Kasaravalli asserts regarding the categorization of Indian cinema. Kasaravalli's statement, "It is not right to brand films made in different languages as Indian cinema as the culture and politics vary in regions. The whole notion of Indian cinema is wrong and it has to be called "Indian cinemas," shows the need to critically assess the term "Indian cinema" as a monolithic construct. His argument hinges on the premise that the vast and diverse cultural landscape of India, comprising numerous languages, traditions, social structures, and political realities, cannot be adequately represented through a singular cinematic lens. (Mathrubhumi, 2024). By calling for the term "Indian cinemas," Kasaravalli suggests the pluralism that characterizes film production across India. This perspective acknowledges that each regional cinema not only reflects local narratives and issues but also engages with its own unique audience sensibilities. For instance, the thematic and stylistic approaches in Kannada cinema, as championed by Kasaravalli himself, differ significantly from those found in Bengali cinema, Malayalam cinema or Assamese cinema. Each genre has distinct cultural expressions, and thus, to homogenize them under a single classification loses the richness and complexity of regional identities. Kasaravalli not only questions traditional classification but also supports inclusivity by advocating "Indian cinemas" rather than "Indian cinema," so acknowledging the significance of regional identities in determining the course of Indian film.

Pabung Aribam strongly asserts, "Indian cinema is not only Bollywood or films with feel-good story line. We have films dealing with real- life in different regions, different cultures of our country. Such films need to be seen by the rest of the country. Diversity is the beauty of Indian culture" (PTI). Pabung's conviction that Indian films consist of their regional cinemas shows a profound understanding of the complicated scenario that shapes the setting of Indian films. He argues that the richness, diversity, and complexity of Indian cinema can only be appreciated when seen through the lens of its various regional expressions.

India is home to a multitude of languages, cultures, and traditions, each with its own storytelling practices and cinematic expressions. Regional cinemas are the vital repositories of local culture, that allow filmmakers to explore specific social issues, traditions, and narratives. Regional films contribute significantly to the national identity of Indian cinema. They provide a platform for regional voices that enrich the collective narrative of the nation. For instance, Bengali cinema has produced influential filmmakers like Satyajit Ray, Ritwik Ghatak and Mrinal Sen, who deal with themes of poverty, identity, and the human condition. Their films, while deeply rooted in Bengali culture, possess universal themes that resonate beyond regional boundaries.

Several filmmakers tell their stories without the constraints of mainstream commercial cinema. This has led to a resurgence of unique narratives drawn from local experiences. Films like *Court* (2014) directed by Chaitanya Tamhane, have won critical acclaim for the portrayal of social issues within the context of Marathi culture. Such films explain how regional cinema can challenge societal norms.

However, a close examination of Pabung's films reveals that his films frequently use a contemplative and subtle storytelling technique, which might not fit the mainstream expectations of Indian film. His career is marked by numerous National and International Film Awards that acknowledge his artistic gift and contributions to cinema.

The academic discourse surrounding Indian cinema has historically concentrated on a select group of filmmakers and their works, often side-lining the significant contributions made by filmmakers such as Aribam Syam Sharma. This selective focus can be attributed to various factors, including the influence of Bollywood. By focusing primarily on filmmakers and films from Bollywood, scholars risk overlooking the rich stories and perspectives that regional cinema offers. This omission has several implications. By centering discussions around Bollywood and its filmmakers, the academic discourse constructs a narrow understanding of Indian cinema. It continues a monolithic view while ignoring the multifaceted nature of storytelling across different cultures and languages within India. Moreover, the lack of scholarly attention to regional filmmakers diminishes the visibility of diverse voices and narratives. Filmmakers like Pabung bring forth local histories, struggles, and cultural tones that are vital for an understanding of Indian society as a whole. Their works often challenge dominant narratives and offer alternative viewpoints that reflect their specific audiences.

Regional cinema, in other words 'Indian cinema', plays a crucial role in preserving and promoting cultural heritage. "In the vast tapestry of Indian cinema, regional films have long been the unsung heroes, quietly making their mark on audiences and industry alike. While Bollywood often dominates the national and international spotlight, the emergence and ascent of regional cinema have been nothing short of a cultural renaissance. From the verdant landscapes of Kerala to the bustling streets of Bengal, from the rugged terrain of Punjab to the serene backwaters of Tamil Nadu, regional cinema has carved out its niche, celebrating the diversity and richness of India's cultural landscape" (Academic Block, 2024). Films that emphasise local traditions, dialects, and issues offer audiences with a sense of identity and belonging. The value of cultural diversity in cinematic landscapes is diminished when these contributions are disregarded. The study of regional filmmakers can enrich academic discourse by incorporating interdisciplinary perspectives, such as anthropology, sociology, and postcolonial studies. This broader approach can enhance the understanding of how cinema interacts with social dynamics, power structures, and identity politics. Analyzing the works of regional filmmakers like Aribam Syam Sharma is essential for a holistic appreciation of Indian cinema, its cultural significance, and the myriad voices that contribute to its richness.

In 2016, we had a long discussion at Itanagar, Arunachal Pradesh, and I was struck by his articulate reflections on his journey as a filmmaker. He said that his initial passion lay not in cinema but in music, a medium that significantly influenced his artistic sensibilities. This discovery shows the interaction between music and film in his works, as he frequently incorporates indigenous musical forms into his films. His background in Rabindra Sangeet, coupled with his understanding of traditional Manipuri music, presents his approach to storytelling. His observations also demonstrated his dedication to understanding the subtleties of Manipuri society through his films. He expressed a desire to portray the everyday lives of ordinary people of the region. Audiences can relate to this emphasis on the common man since it questions accepted stories that sometimes ignore the actual experiences of marginalized communities. In reflecting on my interview with Pabung, it became evident that his contributions to Indian cinema extend far beyond the films he has directed. Supporting a more inclusive and representative portrayal of India's varied cultural scenario, his work questions the dominant narratives inside mainstream cinema.

Pabung Aribam's vast body of work has greatly shaped the scene of regional filmmaking, especially in Manipur. His films are cultural reflections that capture the sociocultural dynamics of Manipuri society, not only artistic statements. With a filmography that includes fifteen feature films and thirty-one non-feature films, along with musical scores for 25 films, his contributions to cinema are both prolific and varied. His notable works, *Imagi Ningthem* (My Son, My Precious, 1981) and *Ishanou* (The Chosen One, 1991), are mentioned as two of the 100 greatest Indian films, marking significant milestones in the history of Indian cinema. *Imagi Ningthem*, recognized for its narrative simplicity and lyrical quality, portrays the profound themes of unconditional love and societal norms through the lens of a woman's relationship with her husband's illegitimate child. The film's pioneering use of a 16mm Bolex camera is representative of Pabung's innovative spirit. It not only won the third national award for him but also gained international acclaim. It travelled prestigious film festivals across the globe and winning the Grand Prix at the Festival des Trois Continents in Nantes, France, in 1982. This accolade marked a watershed moment for Indian cinema, as it was the first Indian film to win such a prestigious award, thereby putting Manipuri cinema on the global map.

Once *Imagi Ningthem* proved successful, the environment around Manipuri film became charged with hope. In 1991, Pabung's *Ishanou* set his reputation as an internationally recognized filmmaker. Its selection for the *Un Certain Regard* section at the Cannes Film Festival showed his ability to transcend regional boundaries. The film's selection in numerous international festivals, including Rotterdam, Toronto, and Tokyo, proves its global appeal.

In recognition of his artistic achievements, Pabung has got recognition, including fifteen national awards, six for feature films and nine for non-feature films. This remarkable achievement not only shows his artistic excellence but also reflects the significance of his contributions to the broader landscape of Indian cinema. Rather than being watched exclusively as entertainment, his films are often subjects of scholarly analysis. The retrospective titled "A Tribute to Aribam Syam Sharma's Cinematic Journey: ...And Miles to Go" at the 38th International Film Festival of India

(IFFI) in Goa in 2007 is an example of how his work has been celebrated and contextualized within the broader scope of Indian cinema. In 1997, the Berkeley Art Museum & Pacific Film Archive at the University of California organized special screenings of Aribam's films. The inclusion of his films in academic and cultural institutions like Berkeley shows a scholarly interest in his contributions. The 6th Mumbai International Film Festival (MIFF) in 2000, which featured a retrospective of his documentaries, and the 7th Dhaka International Film Festival in 2002, which also screened his work, explain the growing appreciation for his unique narrative style and thematic focus. Also, institutions such as the Centre for Film Culture in Assam and the Guwahati Cine Club, in collaboration with the Assam Cine Art Society, have recognized his contributions through their retrospectives. The 6th International Film Festival of Thrissur, Kerala, in 2009, and the 46th International Film Festival of India in 2015, which screened his films, prove the sustained interest in Pabung's work. Moreover, the 9th International Documentary and Short Film Festival of Kerala in 2016, which included a retrospective section dedicated to his films, supports the notion that his work transcends conventional cinematic norms. His documentaries, such as *Monpas of Arunachal Pradesh*, *Orchids of Manipur*, and *Dances of Lai Haraoba*, which were screened at the Yamagata International Documentary Film Festival in 2019, illustrate his versatility as a filmmaker and his commitment to documenting and preserving cultural narratives.

As the Chairman of the Jury for the Indian Panorama at the International Film Festival of India (IFFI) on multiple occasions, specifically in 1997 and 2015 for feature films, and in 2005 and 2009 for non-feature films, Pabung has played a crucial role in promoting Manipuri/Indian cinema on an international stage. In addition to his work with IFFI, his role as Chairman of the Jury for the International Short Film Competition at the Short Film Centre in Goa in 2008 shows his encouragement for the emerging filmmakers.

In 2006, the Government of India honoured Aribam with the Padma Shri, the fourth highest civilian award in the country. Two years later, in 2008, he received the Dr. V. Shantaram Lifetime Achievement Award, conferred by the Ministry of Information and Broadcasting, Government of India, specifically for his contributions to short and documentary filmmaking. Regionally, the Government of Manipur bestowed upon him the "Manipur State Lifetime Achievement Award" in 2000. In 2014, the Brahmaputra Valley Film Festival in Assam acknowledged his enduring legacy by awarding him with a Lifetime Achievement Award. In 2015, the Manipur State Film Development Society and the Film Forum Manipur conferred upon Aribam the title "Jewel of Manipuri Cinema." Pabung has been conferred the Golden Beaver Award, 2025, which is a

Life Time Achievement Award, along with acclaimed actor, Kamal Hassan, at the India Film Festival of Alberta, Canada on 7 September, 2025.

Three remarkable documentaries have been made on Pabung Aribam, each providing a unique perspective on his life and work. The first documentary, titled *Aribam Syam Sharma*, was both scripted and directed by Gurumayum Nirmal Sharma. Produced by Th. Brajabidhu and presented by Doordarshan, this film offers a comprehensive biographical sketch of Aribam Syam Sharma, that speaks of his early life, influence, and the milestones of his illustrious career in cinema. The second documentary, *Pabung Syam* (2020) and directed by Haobam Paban Kumar, focuses on both the personal and professional life of Aribam Syam Sharma. Produced by the Films Division of India, this film explores significant themes and events that have shaped his filmmaking journey. The third documentary, *Aribam Syam Sharma- Laparoscopic Cinemascapes (*2022) and directed by Joshy Joseph, examines the philosophical footings of Pabung's work. The film explores his narrative approach, artistic vision, and how he has enhanced cinema through a unique perspective, giving audiences a better understanding of the films' deeper meanings.

When taken as a whole, these documentaries honour Aribam Syam Sharma's legacy and offer a comprehensive look at his life, work, and influence on Indian cinema. His films, which are firmly rooted in Manipur's cultural identity, are more than just stories;

they are insightful commentary on the state of humanity. Both audiences and aspiring filmmakers are still influenced and inspired by his work as a composer and filmmaker.

Pabung Aribam: A Guiding Light for Filmmakers

Many filmmakers in the North-East draw inspiration from him, not just for his cinematic excellence but also for his rooted lifestyle. He avoids the glitz and glamour often associated with the film industry, choosing instead to focus on his craft and the stories he wants to tell. His down-to-earth nature has earned him respect and admiration, making him a role model for filmmakers who wish to stay true to their roots.

Emerging filmmakers in the region frequently regard Pabung Aribam as a source of inspiration. Pabung's works encourage them to embrace their unique perspectives and share their narratives through film. In a world where mainstream cinema often overshadows regional stories, Pabung Aribam's commitment to Manipuri cinema symbolises hope for many. In addition to his films, Pabung Aribam is also known for his dedication to nurturing new talent. He often holds workshops and mentoring sessions for young filmmakers. This commitment to fostering the next generation of storytellers reflects his belief in the power of cinema to promote understanding among different cultures.

Pabung's legacy is not just about the films he has made but also the impact he has made on the filmmaking community in the North-East. Many others have followed in his footsteps thanks in part to his ability to combine art with authenticity. As more young filmmakers emerge, they carry forward his vision of storytelling that honours their heritage. Through his work and his life, he reminds us all of the beauty of storytelling and the importance of staying connected to our roots.

In a recent conversation with Haobam Paban Kumar of Manipur, acclaimed for his debut feature film *Loktak Lairembee* (Lady of the Lake), which received the National Film Award for Best Film on Environment Conservation/Preservation at the 64th National Film Awards in 2017 and the German Star of India at the 14th Indian Film Festival in Stuttgart, Germany, reflects on his experiences with Pabung Aribam. Haobam Paban states, "My teacher and filmmaker Pabung Aribam Syam Sharma- the father of Manipuri cinema is a legend. My real film education started from Pabung's sets- how to clap, write continuity sheet, always check the frame from behind the camera, lensing, trolley movement, how to hold a reflector, how to handle the actors etc. But one thing that had a profound impact on me and my work is discipline. I realize that without discipline you can never make films there is so much money and manpower involved while making a film. I was always fascinated by the realistic approach of Pabung, working with non-actors, real locations etc. When I made my first fiction feature in 2016 people were talking about the blurring line between fiction and non-fiction which Pabung had done long time back in his films like *Imagi Ningthem* and *Ishanou*."

Bobo Khuraijam off Manipur, whose documentary *Ima Sabitri* (2018) premiered at Indian Panorama (Non-Feature Section), worked with Pabung in various roles, including assistant director, scriptwriter, and actor. In a personal conversation, he speaks of Pabung Aribam, "I don't know how much Pabung has influenced me as a filmmaker, but I do know that his approach to life and cinema is no different. It wouldn't be wrong to say that Pabung is someone who is constantly in awe of the world around him, not because he finds it unfathomable. He observes, reads, and ponders, yet he is not easily satisfied with answers that claim to be definitive. For instance, Pabung made *Ishanou* (1990) after documenting *Lai Haraoba* with more than fifty hours of footage. But Pabung will never claim to know anything about *Lai Haraoba* or the *Maibis*. On another occasion, during the editing of *Sankirtana, ritual singing, drumming and dancing of Manipur* (2013), Pabung would ask, "Why does rhythm arouse us?" To this day, he must have found many probable answers to his question about rhythm. Yet I am sure a singular answer will not suffice for his inquiry. I believe this particular approach is well reflected in his films as well. This unique trait of Pabung is something I will constantly try to imbibe."

Bobby Wahengbam, a national award-winning film critic from Manipur, said during our conversation that India is known for its privileged political, social, and cultural gift—unity in diversity. Wahengbam holds the belief that Indian cinema covers cinema from every corner of the country. Bollywood and its style of classist cinema are, no doubt, a global phenomenon. At the same time, Indian cinema is also synonymous with Satyajit Ray. Wahengbam asserts that, similar to Ray, Pabung Aribam is an iconic Manipuri filmmaker whose films have the potential to leave a lasting impact in the global cinema landscape. It is indeed a celebration if an Indian cinema wins at Nantes and makes an official entry to Cannes since such achievements are rare in our cinema history. Aribam's *Imagi Ningthem* (1981) won the Golden Montgolfier at Nantes, and *Ishanou* (1990) enjoyed official entry into Cannes and is considered a classic by Cannes recently. Wahengbam states that Pabung's success on such prestigious cinema platforms is particularly significant, given that his films were produced despite significant challenges, such as the absence of a visible film industry in his area of expertise. Yet, through his school, filmmakers from Manipur like Haobam Paban Kumar, Sanzu Bachaspatimayum, Ronel Haobam, and cinematographer Irom Maipak emerged to make a mark in the global scenario. He expresses concern that the exclusion of Pabung from the roster of pioneers of Indian cinema will undoubtedly signify a neglect of our cinematic heritage and the fundamental principle of national identity rooted in unity amidst diversity.

Wahengbam's concern regarding Pabung Aribam's exclusion from the canon of Indian cinema's pioneers indicates a broader issue of historiography and cultural memory. It suggests that neglecting such figures risks erasing significant contributions to the nation's collective artistic heritage. It raises vital questions about who is deemed a "pioneer" and the criteria for inclusion in national narratives. It emphasizes the need for a more inclusive approach to documenting and celebrating the diverse cinematic landscape of India. In his speech, Wahengbam asks for a re-evaluation of the past of Indian cinema and emphasises the basic idea of national identity that which results from appreciating its variety. This reflective involvement not only honours the legacy of directors like Aribam but also questions the dominant narratives that sometimes give particular genres or regions top priority, so reaffirming the great complexity and depth of Indian film as a whole.

Meena Longjam is a distinguished documentary filmmaker from Manipur and is recognised as the first woman filmmaker from the region to receive a National Award for her debut documentary film, *Auto Driver* (2016). Pabung Aribam, according to Longjam, was her inspiration. She says, "We revered to him lovingly as Pabung Aribam Syam Sharma. He is a cultural doyen and a pioneering filmmaker from Manipur. His work, starting from

Matamgi Manipur to *Ishanou*, and his one of the well-regarded documentaries, *Yelhou Jagoi*, inspires me as a filmmaker in many ways. His exponential works and dedication to telling stories that reflect our cultural nuances and aesthetics and our traditions and struggles resonates deeply with me. The collaboration of Pabung Syam and the late Maharaj Kumari Binodini of Manipur led to various phenomenal works that remained masterpieces *(Ishanou, The Chosen One) and* even entered the World Classic in Cannes in 2023.

"What I, as an academician and filmmaker, admire most about his work is his commitment to showcasing the rich cultural heritage of Manipur while also addressing social issues and human emotions. His films have been a timeless quality to us. I believe his legacy continues to inspire many a new generation of filmmakers. As a filmmaker, I would strive to learn from his approach to storytelling, his attention to details, and his passion for showcasing the beauty and complexity of our region, Manipur. His influence encourages me to explore themes and stories that are meaningful to my community while pushing the boundaries of cinematic storytelling," said Longjam.

Beyond the Boundary

Pabung Aribam's influence extends beyond the confines of Manipuri cinema. Pradip Kurbah, who brought Meghalayan cinema to the world map when he won the prestigious Kim Ji-seok Award at the 24th Busan International Film Festival (BIFF) in Korea for his film *Iewduh* (Market), asserts: "Aribam Shyam Sharma sir's vision has guided my filmmaking journey from the very start. His skill at portraying cultural details showed me the value of telling stories authentically. By watching his films, I learnt how vital it is to preserve local traditions on screen. He brought a revolution to Manipuri cinema, yet he remains strangely overlooked on the national stage. Despite his immense contributions, Indian cinema discussions rarely credit him as a pioneer. While rooted in Manipuri culture, his films touch on universal truths that speak to everyone. His impact lives on in every filmmaker who wants to create honest, culturally grounded stories. His legacy shows the richness of Indian cinema and deserves much wider appreciation."

In his reflection on the contributions of Pabung to the landscape of Indian cinema, Kurbah expresses a profound recognition of the cultural and artistic significance of Pabung's work. He states, "His skill at portraying cultural details showed me the value of telling stories authentically," which focuses the transformative power that an authentic narrative holds in representing marginalized voices. Kurbah's acknowledgment of Pabung's influence focuses on a important pedagogical relationship common in the realm of cinema, whereby established auteurs provide a foundational blueprint for emerging filmmakers. The emphasis on "telling stories authentically" renders the act of filmmaking as not merely a technical work but a cultural responsibility. Kurbah's assertion that "he brought a revolution to Manipuri cinema" offers the notion of Pabung as a pioneering figure whose cinematic contributions have irrevocably altered the course of regional cinema. Kurbah's lament that Pabung Aribam remains "strangely overlooked on the national stage" proves as a critique of the national cinema discourse. It reveals the systemic marginalization of regional narratives within the broader Indian cinematic canon.

Kurbah's disappointment, expressed in the phrase "a major figure in regional cinema has not been fully acknowledged," reflects the ongoing challenges faced by filmmakers who operate within regional contexts but whose works resonate with larger cultural and existential concerns. Kurbah situates Pabung Aribam's legacy within the larger narrative of Indian cinema's richness, noting that "his films touch on universal truths that speak to everyone." As Kurbah states, "His legacy shows the richness of Indian cinema and deserves much wider appreciation," capturing the urgent need for a paradigm shift towards a more equitable acknowledgment of diverse cinematic voices.

Another remarkable filmmaker from Meghalaya, Dominic Sangma, has garnered attention for his film *Rapture* (2023), which premiered at the prestigious 76th Locarno Film Festival on August 10, 2023, in the Concorso Cineasti del presente section. Following its successful debut, *Rapture* received a warm reception in France, premiering at the Festival des 3 Continents in Nantes on May 15, 2024. In a personal conversation with Sangma, he expressed admiration for Aribam Syam Sharma, stating, "I haven't had the opportunity to watch many of his films, apart from *Ishanou.* However, I hold Aribam Syam Sharma in very high regard as a filmmaker. I've read extensively about him and heard numerous discussions surrounding his work, which is known for its profound philosophical themes." This sentiment reflects Sangma's respect for Pabung's contributions to cinema and the impact of his thought-provoking storytelling.

Veteran filmmaker from Nagaland, Kivini Shohe states, "Aribam Syam Sharma's films are captivating to me because of the nuanced exploration of human emotions and relationships. His films are a testament to his innovative spirit, cinematic vision, and commitment to telling stories that matter, offering a unique window into the lives and traditions of the people of Manipur. Despite limited resources, Pabung Aribam has consistently pushed the boundaries, finding creative solutions to technical and logistical challenges. The North-Eastern region has historically been neglected by the central government and mainstream media, leading to a lack of representation and recognition. This may be one of the reasons his films, despite their critical acclaim and contributions, have not received due recognition in India" (personal communication, 30 April, 2024).

Shohe's insights into Pabung's films enlighten a persuasive dichotomy between artistic merit and the systemic neglect that characterizes the representation of Northeast India in the broader national discourse. His films resonate as a "testament to his innovative spirit, cinematic vision, and commitment to telling stories that matter," which prompts a re-evaluation of what constitutes significant cinema in a multicultural nation like India. Yet, within this celebration of Pabung's originality lies a troubling reality. The very essence of his work is inextricably linked to the identity and struggles of the people of Manipur, a region that has remained largely marginalized in the context of Indian cinema. This marginalization can be linked to a historical oversight by both the central government and mainstream media. The lack of acknowledgment for his contributions, despite their "critical acclaim," suggests a broader systemic failure to appreciate the cultural traces and narratives that filmmakers from marginalized regions bring to the national stage.

Napo RZ Thanga, a filmmaker from Mizoram, is recognised for his documentary titled *MNF: The Mizo Uprising* (2014). He praises Pabung Aribam, remarking, "I have watched only one film, *Ishanou*, yet I consider him to be an outstanding filmmaker. He adeptly conveys the complexities of human emotions through exceptional cinematic excellence."

National award winning filmmaker from Assam, Suraj Dowarah asserts that the works of

Pabung Aribam remain largely overlooked within the broader landscape of Indian cinema, attributable to several contributing factors. Initially, Dowarah suggests that Indian cinema is fundamentally categorised into two principal segments: Hindi and South Indian, with some notable exceptions for Bengali films. This classification arises from the aggressive tendencies observed in the romanticised depictions of melodrama, music, sexuality, and violence, which are frequently associated with the mainstream films featuring prominent stars. Conversely, Aribam sir's films exhibit a minimalistic approach, characterised by profound thematic discourse that often diverges from the conventional preferences of the average cine-goer. Also, cinephiles often lack familiarity with the unique cultural ethos and ethnic diversity of the North East, particularly Manipur, distinguishing it from the rest of the nation, and cinema reflects this gap in understanding. As a filmmaker, I greatly admire Pabung for his ability to approach local subjects with a universal perspective. (personal communication, Nov 30, 2024).

Young filmmaker and research scholar Aditya Modak of Tripura writes in his article, "Aribam Syam Sharma's Immense Contribution to Indian Cinema Remains Relatively Unsung": "One name inseparably linked with Manipuri cinema is that of Aribam Syam Sharma. For as long as Manipuri cinema (or Northeast Indian cinema for that matter) continues to be discussed, Aribam Syam Sharma will always be regarded as one of the most influential filmmakers who not only shaped Manipuri cinema, giving it a unique identity, but also took it to international platforms, garnering worldwide acclaim. Despite his magnanimous contribution to the field of cinema, there have not been much intensive scholarly works done on Syam Sharma in the mainstream academic fields of Film Studies or Cultural Studies, and his works remain relatively underappreciated in mainstream media and academia" (Modak, 2023).

In recent years, there has been a growing chorus of voices from both filmmakers and film critics expressing disappointment over the omission of Aribam Syam Sharma from receiving the Dadasaheb Phalke Award. Critics argue that the Dadasaheb Phalke Award should honour filmmakers who have not only excelled in their craftsmanship but have also contributed to the conservation and promotion of regional cinema. Considered a pioneer in this regard, Pabung Aribam's works have often showcased the rich culture and traditions of Manipuri society. By not acknowledging his contributions with the Dadasaheb Phalke Award, many believe that the essence and values of the award are being undermined. They contend that it reflects a broader issue of the marginalization of regional cinema within the national narrative of Indian filmmaking.

In a personal communication with the national award-winning filmmaker and critic, Utpal Borpujari expresses that Aribam Syam Sharma is a true living legend of Indian cinema, and every serious film enthusiast in the country would admit that. He has been synonymous with the cinema of Manipur since the time Manipuri cinema took birth in 1972. He has made acclaimed fiction and non-fiction films that form his enviable oeuvre and is, to date, the only filmmaker from Northeast India to have a feature film in the official selection of the Cannes Film Festival (*Ishanou*, Un Certain Regard, 1991). Borpujari stresses that he is a filmmaker who truly deserves the Dadasaheb Phalke Award, the highest honour in Indian cinema. But sadly, when film scholars and critics discuss legends of Indian cinema, only a few remember to mention him. It seems the "Mainland" is still unable to focus its spotlight on a filmmaker from the far east of India. The recent restoration of the print of *Ishanou* by the Film Heritage Foundation and its screening at the Cannes Classics section, followed by a few other prominent festivals, briefly made the film world remember his name. Borpujari continues that the fact remains that, unlike many of the masters who emerged during the 1970s, Pabung Aribam's cinema remains in the shadows, despite the fact that his filmmaking continued until some years ago. Perhaps this has to do with the fact that cinema made in the 'bigger' languages is discussed and consumed more by both film critics/scholars and common cinegoers, while those made in 'smaller' languages in far corners of the country continue to remain in the shadows. Borpujari stressed that Pabung Aribam deserves to receive the Dadasaheb Phalke Award and the government should seriously consider bestowing him with the honour. We should widely celebrate his cinema that is strongly rooted in Manipuri society and culture, yet are universal stories about humanity and empathy.

I would like to mention here two names: film critic, Shoma A. Chatterji, and National Award-winning filmmaker from Kerala, Joshy Joseph. Notably, although neither Chatterji nor Joseph comes from the North-East region, both have expressed their concern and frustration over the inadequate recognition given to Aribam's films, particularly emphasized by the omission of the prestigious Dadasaheb Phalke Award. Through their positive evaluations of Pabung Aribam's body of work, they believe that this omission is likely due to the systemic biases against marginalized regions like Manipur, rather than any shortcomings in the artistic quality of his films. Calcutta based film critic Shoma A. Chatterji writes in her article, "Aribam Syam Sharma: A Man in Search of The Manipuri Identity" that the raging question raised by filmmaker Joshy Joseph is "why is Aribam Syam Sharma being brushed under the carpet when it comes to selecting a film celebrity for the Dadasaheb Phalke Award"? Is it because Pabung Aribam is from the North East, an area marginalized deliberately by all and sundry linked to prestigious awards in the country? Or, is it because he prefers to live a low-key life away from the hullabaloo of celebrity circuses rampant in the media? Perhaps, it is a blend of both considering that he has kept away from the Dadasaheb Phalke Award though he has won 19 National Awards and umpteen international awards over time (Chatterji, 2023).

Chatterji's analysis of Pabung Aribam's cinematic contributions is enlightened by the inquiry posed by filmmaker Joshy Joseph. It shows the inherent biases present within the established frameworks of the Indian film industry. Joseph's inquiry into the conspicuous exclusion of Pabung Aribam from the esteemed Dadasaheb Phalke Award, despite his remarkable array of national and international accolades, suggests the complex layers of marginalisation faced by artists hailing from the North East. His observation indicates that Pabung Aribam's geographic and cultural background, originating from a region frequently positioned at the margins, plays a substantial role in this marginalisation. Joseph's observation regarding Pabung's inclination towards a "low-key life" rather than participating in the "hullabaloo of celebrity circuses" is in fact, a commentary on the commodification of art and the pervasive celebrity culture that characterises the film industry. Joseph's inquiry not only expresses Pabung's personal narrative but also acts as an effective call to re-evaluate the frameworks that shape artistic recognition within the national discourse.

The debate over the award raises important questions about how contributions to cinema are recognized and valued. For as long as Manipuri cinema (or North-East or Indian cinema for that matter) continues to be discussed, Aribam Syam

Sharma will always be regarded as one of the most influential filmmakers who not only shaped Manipuri cinema, giving it a unique identity, but also took it to international platforms, garnering worldwide acclaim.

Pabung Aribam has significantly influenced the representation of indigenous narratives and the socio-cultural dynamics of marginalised communities, especially in the North-East. By emphasising local narratives and using indigenous aesthetics, Aribam advocates for a comprehensive portrayal of Manipur's cultural heritage. However, his exclusion from such awards prompts significant enquiries regarding the criteria employed to evaluate merit within the Indian cinematic sphere. Do these metrics truly signify a sincere recognition of diversity, or do they merely reinforce the prevailing hierarchies within the cinematic landscape? This study shows a more extensive systemic concern: the disregard for regional perspectives and the historical neglect of contributions from under represented areas such as Manipur.

For Pabung, the accolades and awards, whether they are national, international, or even the prestigious Dadasaheb Phalke Award, are not his primary concern. He is scarcely excited by the recognition that comes with receiving such distinctions. Instead, what motivates him most is his deep commitment to the art of Manipuri cinema.

Pabung chooses to live a private life and stays away from the chaos of celebrity culture. In a world where many seek validation through fame, Pabung's commitment to his craft is a reminder of how happiness comes from following your passion and being honest. More than any awards, he cares about how his work affects people and how honest it is.

***

Works Cited

Modak, A. (2023, April 29). Aribam Syam Sharma's immense contribution to Indian cinema remains relatively unsung – Imphal Review of Arts and Politics. https://imphalreviews.in/aribam-syam-sharmas-immense-contribution-to-indian-cinema-remains-relatively-unsung/

Chatterji, S. A. (2023, October 29). Aribam Syam Sharma: A man in search of the Manipuri Identity - The Space Ink. *thespace.ink*. https://thespace.ink/books-culture/books-movies-music/aribam-syam-sharma-a-man-in-search-of-the-manipuri-identity/

Pickle. (2018, April 12). No Indian Film Should be Tagged as Regional Film: Adoor Gopalakrishnan. Pickle Media - Pickle Media Entertainment India. https://pickle.co.in/film/no-indian-film-should-be-tagged-as-regional-film-adoor-gopalakrishnan/

Academic Block. (2024, December 25). *Regional Cinema | Academic Block*. https://www.academicblock.com/life-and-leisure/history-of-indian-cinema/regional-cinema

The Times of India. (2018, December 25). Respect for regional cinema key, says noted filmmaker Jahnu Barua. *The Times of India.* https://timesofindia.indiatimes.com/city/pune/respect-for-regional-cinema-key-says-noted-filmmaker-jahnu-barua/articleshow/67237071.cms

Mathrubhumi. (2024, January 6). Not right to look at Indian cinema as one cultural entity: Girish Kasaravalli. *English.Mathrubhumi.* https://english.mathrubhumi.com/movies-music/news/not-right-to-look-at-indian-cinema-as-one-cultural-entity-says-girish-kasaravalli-1.9216951

"Indian Cinema Is Not Bollywood: Aribam Syam Sharma." *The Indian Express*, 24 Nov. 2015, indianexpress.com/article/entertainment/bollywood/indian-cinema-is-not-bollywood-aribam-syam-sharma.

Chapter One

Cinema of Manipur:

A Symphony of Struggle and Hope

Nestled in the lush landscape of North-East India, Manipur, which translates to "a land of jewel", is a state famous for its charming beauty and rich history. This region is home to diverse cultures, vibrant traditions, and breath-taking natural scenery, including the famous Loktak Lake, the largest freshwater lake in India. Visitors to Manipur are often fascinated by its festival, traditional dance forms, and the warm hospitality of its people. Manipur is bordered by Nagaland to the north, Mizoram to the south, and Assam to the west, while its eastern and southern boundaries are shared with the international territory of Myanmar (formerly Burma). Imphal, the vibrant capital, is situated at the heart of this picturesque state, which once thrived as a princely kingdom involved in numerous territorial disputes with its neighbour, Burma.

The history of modern Manipur unfolds weaving together the saga of resilience from the tumultuous era of the *Seven Years' Devastation* through the shadow of the Burmese Empire to the present day. Among the numerous incursions, the most significant took place in 1819, under the reign of King Marjit, when the Burmese forces laid claim to Manipur. This occupation cast a long shadow over the land, persisting until 1826, shaping the indomitable spirit of its people.

In the article "The Seven Years Devastation (1819 -1826) in Manipur," Maibam Chanu Babiya offers a profound exploration of a period known as *Chahi Taret Khuntakpa* (The Seven Years Devastation), marked by the Burmese dominion that wreaked significant havoc in the valley of Manipur between 1819 and 1826. This catastrophic epoch, commencing on the 12th day in 1819 and concluding in February 1826, is often regarded as the darkest chapter in Manipur's history, with lasting repercussions on its political, social, and economic landscape. The Burmese military campaigns during this time were characterized by brutal acts of torture and systematic plunder, subjecting the Manipuri populace to profound suffering that has left indelible scars in the collective memory of the community. Citing Dr. N. Birachandra's poignant observation in his work *Seven Years Devastation: 1819-1826*, Babiya explains that this episode will forever be remembered by the Manipuris (Meiteis) as an unforgivingly deep wound, evoking memories of the violence and dehumanization inflicted by the Burmese.

Babiya states that the roots of the *Seven Years Devastation* can be traced back to the tumultuous political dynamics that evolved from the reign of Maharaj Garibniwaj (1709-1748) through to Maharaj Marjit (1813-1819). The dysfunctions of Manipur's governance can largely be attributed to Garibniwaj's reckless decisions, including the destruction of invaluable Puyas (manuscripts), which not only represented the cultural heritage of Manipuri society but also the complex political succession that arose from his decision to elevate his incompetent son, Chit Shai, to the throne over the rightful heir, Shyam Shai. This pivotal blunder caused a war of succession among his descendants, making a chasm in the political stability that had been carefully cultivated by Garibniwaj and his predecessors. The resulting instability from the constant shifts in power severely undermined the integrity of the political framework he had established. Rather than fortifying the kingdom against external threats, many of the ruling successors succumbed to indulgence, prioritizing personal pleasures over the defense of their homeland, leaving Manipur vulnerable to the impending Burmese onslaught.

Babiya asserts that Manipur's political disarray allowed the Burmese to rise ascendant under the ambitious leadership of King Alungpaya (1754-1763), who was relentless in his vision of unifying Burma through a series of sweeping social and political reforms. His military was effectively reorganized, fortified by modern weaponry, rendering Burma a formidable adversary in stark contrast to the beleaguered Manipuri forces. The imperative for a united Burma, fuelled by imperialistic ambition, positioned them advantageously over the Manipuris, ultimately leading to the calamitous events of 1819-

1826. The immediate catalyst for this invasion was Marjit's refusal to attend the coronation of Bagidaw, the king of Burma. After ascending the throne of Manipur in 1813, with assistance from the Burmese, Marjit was initially subservient, surrendering the Kabaw Valley and compromising the kingdom's independence. When Bagidaw issued the order for Marjit to attend his coronation, Marjit's refusal incited the Burmese king's ire, prompting a military response that culminated in a brutal invasion. The Burmese forces systematically decimated the Manipuri armies, committing egregious acts of violence against the populace, indiscriminately slaughtering men, women, and children, and laying waste to the valley. Women and children suffered unimaginable horrors, including being confined in ventilated spaces and subjected to smoke-induced deaths due to burning chilies, while men captured during the conflict were brutally tortured and forced into servitude—a harrowing reminder of the height of human cruelty. In response to the Burmese oppression, a Manipuri prince named Herachandra emerged as a beacon of resistance. Differing from his contemporaries, who fled to Cachar, he rallied the remaining Manipuris, forming a revolutionary cohort of 800 individuals in March 1820. Embracing guerrilla tactics, he orchestrated attacks against the Burmese forces, achieving notable successes, particularly through the collaboration of Manipuri women. His audacious infiltration of Burmese camps culminated in a daring mission that resulted in the death of numerous enemy soldiers, thereby facilitating subsequent efforts by Gambhir Singh to restore sovereignty to Manipur.

Babiya adds that as tensions escalated among the Manipuri princes exiled in Cachar, Gambhir Singh ultimately emerged as a leader, consolidating power and refocusing efforts on the liberation of Manipur. The British, recognizing the strategic importance of aligning with Gambhir Singh, facilitated an alliance to counter the Burmese threat. Their collaborative efforts culminated in a series of military engagements that led to a successful campaign against the Burmese forces, ultimately resulting in Gambhir Singh's ascension to the throne of Manipur by June 1825. By early 1826, having effectively conquered the Kabaw Valley and restored some semblance of stability, Gambhir Singh's reign continued until the Anglo-Burmese War culminated in the *Treaty of Yandaboo* on February 24, 1826, recognizing him as an independent ruler.

According to the Peberton Report of 1835, Manipur once sprawled across a much larger area than it does now, reflecting the ever-changing dynamics of power throughout its history, especially during the reign of its formidable king, Pamheiba, known to many as Garibaniwaj. Under his leadership, the Manipuris rose to significant prominence, launching several campaigns against the Burmese in the years 1725, 1735, 1738, and 1749, where they emerged victorious, wreaking havoc on Burmese territories.

Yet, in the year 1890, the tides shifted dramatically as Burma initiated its own invasion of Manipur.

During this crisis, King Gambhir Singh sought refuge in Assam's Cachhar district, where he regrouped his forces, with the support of the British, to reclaim his homeland. Yet this relationship soon soured, culminating in a fierce conflict with the British in 1891. The gallant Manipuri warriors, wielding their swords and spears, stood resolute against the might of the well-armed British forces, who brandished their guns with confidence. The decisive battle at Khongjom on April 23, 1891, marked a poignant moment in this struggle; despite their valour, Major Paona and his troops were ultimately defeated, leading to a heavy toll of lives, including that of Paona himself. This day is now observed as "Khongjom Day," a time of remembrance and honour for the sacrifices made during that battle. In the wake of their defeat, the British seized the storied Kangla Palace, culminating in the tragic public executions of Tikendrajit and General Thangal on August 13, 1891. This poignant chapter in history is remembered each year as "Patriot's Day," a solemn tribute to their sacrifice. With these events, Manipur came under British rule (Government of Manipur, n.d.).

In the book *Political Development in Manipur*, author S. M. A. W. Chisthi (2005) poignantly depicts the heart-wrenching public executions of Tikendrajit and General Thangal, capturing the profound sorrow and significance of these historical events. According to Chisthi (2005), Chandra Kirti was succeeded by his son Sur Chandra in May 1886. But his ascendency was challenged by Bara Chauba Singh, the eldest son of Nar. He was not successful and Bara Chauba was taken into custody by Sur Chandra. Sur Chandra was a weak ruler. This encouraged rivalries among his eight brothers, which later resulted in the emergence of two groups. It reached a climax when the group of Tikendrajit attacked the palace in September 1890. The Senapati Tikendrajit and two of his other brothers took possession of the palace. Panicked, Sur Chandra abdicated the throne and sought asylum at the residence of the Political Agent.

Chisthi (2005) notes that Jubraj Kula Chandra Bhaja was installed as the king of Manipur with the assistance of Senapati Tikendrajit, the chief architect of the uprising. The British government recognized the new monarch but harboured resentment towards the Senapati for his actions against the former king. Consequently, a small military force from the Assam government was dispatched to Manipur to implement the orders from the Government of India, which included the arrest of the Senapati. On March 22, 1891, Chief Commissioner Quinton, along with his party, arrived in Imphal. Anticipating British intentions, the Senapati refrained from attending the Durbar held in honour of the British. When the Chief Commissioner attempted to apprehend the Senapati at his residence, severe hostilities erupted, resulting in the brutal murders of Quinton and four of his officers by the Manipuris. The remaining British officers, unable to control the situation, fled to Silchar in Assam. On April 27, 1891, a large military force arrived in Imphal to suppress the Manipuri uprising. The Manipuris were ultimately overpowered, and the Jubraj, Senapati, and other key figures involved in the rebellion were arrested. Tikendrajit was convicted of waging war against the Queen Empress and for abetting the murder of the British officers, leading to his death sentence. He was executed by hanging alongside General Thangal on August 13, 1891 (p. 20-21).

Following the Anglo-Manipur War of 1891, Manipur gracefully rose to the status of a Princely State under the aegis of British rule. Miranda Bembem Mutuwa states in the article, "Colonialism and the Princely state of Manipur: Creation of Modern Urban Space in North-East India" that in 1835, an office of British Agency was set up in Manipur as a sign of friendship between the British and Manipur Kingdom whose primary responsibility was to fend any disputes between the Kingdom of Ava and Manipur. The relationship remained congenial and friendly until British intervention in a palace dispute in 1891, leading to Anglo-Manipur war. This event in the history of Manipur marked the inception of British power in Manipur. After a long debate in the British Parliament, it was decided that Manipur should not be annexed by the colonial power but be maintained as a Princely state under the indirect rule which allowed minimum investment in material and human resource by the British. Manipur was one of the last smallest kingdoms to join the list of Princely states under British Raj. In the hierarchy of princely states, it was given the status of 11-gun salute and remained a Princely state till 1947.

Later on, the area turned into a major conflict area for the Second World War. Among the chaos of World War II, Manipur became a central stage for the Allies' valiantly united resistance against the Japanese advance. It was here that the tide of war turned, with the defeat of Japan preceding the Allies' eventual entry into Imphal, marking a significant juncture in the broader battleground of the time. In the wake of the war, the Manipur Constitution of 1947 was established, marking the dawn of a new democratic era. In this transformative period, the Maharaja was appointed as the elected leader overseeing both the executive and legislative branches. However, the course of history took a decisive turn in 1949 when Maharaja Bodhchandra Singh was summoned to Shillong, the capital of Meghalaya. There he signed an accession treaty, formally tying his kingdom into India's fabric. Following the event, the legislative assembly was dissolved; Manipur formally joined the Republic of India in October of that year. In 1956, Manipur was designated as a united territory, and by 1972, it had achieved the status of a full-fledged state. It was during this transformative period that Mairembam Koireng Singh took office as the first Chief Minister of Manipur State (Government of Manipur, n.d.).

Just before the dawn of independence on 11 August 1947, Maharaja Bodhchandra Singh signed the "Instrument of Accession" with the Indian government, so launching a new chapter for Manipur. He was promised protection of Manipur's autonomy in exchange for his joining the Indian Union. But in response to mounting public opinion, the Maharaja decided to hold elections in June 1948, so establishing a constitutional monarchy. Manipur thus became the first state in India to welcome elections based on universal adult suffrage.

Yet, within the Manipur State Assembly, a divergence of opinion emerged regarding the integration into the Indian Union. While the Manipur Congress advocated for a merger, other political factions expressed their dissent. The Indian government, overlooking the assembly's stance, exerted pressure on the Maharaja to finalize the accession agreement, ultimately achieving the successful integration of Manipur into the Indian Union. On the momentous day of August 15, 1947, Manipur re-established itself as a Sovereign Independent Kingdom. The Maharaja took a pivotal step by enacting the Manipur Constitution Act of 1947, which set the stage for a democratic government, with the Maharaja as the Executive Head, complemented by a newly elected legislative assembly. Yet, this promising era of independence was to be fleeting; on September 21, 1949, Maharaja Bodhchandra signed the agreement to merge with the Union of India, and this led to Manipur's merger into

India on October 15, 1949, bringing the chapter of its independent kingdom to a close.

Wahengbam Pathou (2013) writes in the article, "Biography of His Highness Maharaja Bodhachandra that on 21 September, 1949 Maharaja Bodhchandra appended his royal signature on Merger Agreement. The stroke of His Highness pen on the merger agreement paper dealt a death blow to the sovereignty of Manipur. Committing a tragedy of errors, Maharaja Bodhchandra ceded sovereignty of Manipur to Dominion of India by signing the merger agreement under state of duress. In fact, the merger agreement document was the graveyard of Manipur's sovereignty that Maharaja Bodhchandra was forced to sign under unremitting coercion. On hearing the news that Maharaja Bodhchandra had signed merger agreement, Chief Minister Capt. M.K. Priyabrata convened a session of Manipur Legislative Assembly on 28 September, 1949. Pathou (2013) asserts that the Assembly passed a resolution to denounce the undemocratic and illegal manner in which the Government of India had concluded merger agreement with Maharaja Bodhchandra. The resolution clearly underlined that 'the Assembly will not abide by the agreement' and 'Manipur will have no relation with India'.

In the same article, Pathou (2013) states that curtains came down on the two millennia old institution of monarchy in Manipur on 15 October, 1949. Maharaja Bodhchandra was dispossessed of his royal powers as ruler of Manipur. Government of India abolished institution of monarchy and Maj. Gen. Rawal Amar Singh was made Chief Commissioner of Manipur on the day Manipur was merged to India. Soon after assuming office, Rawal Amar Singh unceremoniously dismissed democratically elected government of Manipur led by Capt. M. K. Priyabrata and dissolved the elected assembly. All the powers vested in the council of ministers and legislative assembly were usurped by the Chief Commissioner. Pathou (2013) emphasises that 15 October, 1949 was a sad day for democracy in Manipur. Dismissal of Capt. M. K. Priyabrata government was travesty of democracy. Dissolution of the elected assembly was bonfire of democracy.

Holden Furber (1951), a professor of South Asia Studies at the University of Pennsylvania, writes, "Effective from 1950, the Constitution of India classified the constituent units of India into three classes—Part A, B, and C states. The former British provinces, together with the princely states that had been merged into them, were the Part A states. The princely unions, plus Mysore and Hyderabad, were the Part B states. The former Chief Commissioners' Provinces and other centrally administered areas, except the Andaman and Nicobar Islands, were the Part C states." From that moment, Manipur became a part of the Indian Union, eventually achieving statehood in 1972.

On January 21, 1972, Manipur gained official status as a state within India under the North Eastern Areas (Regulation) Act of 1971. The state is characterized by remarkable ethnic diversity, comprising 33 officially recognized tribes. The Meitei community, the largest ethnic group, predominantly resides in the capital, Imphal, where the Meitei language, one of India's 22 official languages, is widely spoken. The neighbouring hilly areas are home to the Naga, Kuki-Zo tribes, and other ethnic groups which contribute to the state's vibrant cultural scene, defined by distinct dialects, traditional dress, and customary practices. It has the diverse linguistic, political, and socioeconomic backgrounds, and has endured ethnic conflicts that have produced enduring repercussions. The most extensive of these was the Naga-Kuki conflict, which led to considerable fatalities. The Meiteis have traditionally maintained a legendary connection with the Tangkhul Nagas. The concept of a Greater Nagaland does not conform to this narrative; yet, the Kabui Naga and the Tangkhul Naga of Ukhrul are unequivocally integral to the Meitei perspective. This aspect is crucial for comprehending Pabung Aribam's *Paokhum Ama*, *Ishanou*, and *Lai-Haraoba*, in addition to *Sangai.*

In a personal communication, Pabung Aribam states that he made *Paokhum Ama* in Tangkhul and Meitei. This particular film is political. It deals with the political issue of the region. This is some sort of insurgency, just like Assam. I mean, the youth of our state were not happy about the socio-political scenario and also about the administration of the region. Actually, Manipur was a kingdom until 1949. On midnight 15 August, 1947, Manipur became independent, and up to 1949, they had their assembly. At that time, M.K. Binodini, the Maharani, was the member of the legislative assembly. The assembly members were not chosen through an election but rather appointed by nomination. In 1949, the Government of India appointed a Chief Commissioner (Maj. Gen. Rawal Amar Singh) to lead Manipur as a Part C State. This Chief Commissioner became the ruler of the state. From 1949 to 1972, Manipur was not a state but a Part C state. You know, this was the beginning upsurge of this region, as Manipuris were not content. Some sort of insurgency was coming up. During this period, the youths experienced a lack of job opportunities and expressed dissatisfaction with the overall situation. I was personally affected by this dissatisfaction. But through my songs, I tried to mirror such situations. But in films, only *Paokhum Ama* reflects the mindset of that particular time. In such a socio-political landscape, many youths took arms, and even now, the continuation is there. The film, *Paokhum Ama* (1983), was set in the 1980s."

Tumultuous Times

Manipur is famous for its rich cultural heritage, featuring unique traditional dance forms and athletic practices. Cultural expressions include *Raas Leela*, *Jagoi* (a traditional Manipuri dance), *Pung cholom* (an energetic drumming performance), and *Thang-Ta*, alongside *Sagol Kangei*, a traditional form of polo. However, the state's landscape has been marred by insurgency and the imposition of the Armed Forces (Special Powers) Act (AFSPA), creating a climate of insecurity.

The tumultuous decades of the 1960s and 1970s in Manipur were characterized by a burgeoning insurgency that fundamentally altered the political and sociocultural landscape of the region. This period marked the rise of multiple insurgent groups, notably the Revolutionary Peoples' Front, the People's Liberation Army, the People's Revolutionary Party of Kangleipak, and the Red Army, each imbued with distinct ideological footings and grievances primarily revolving around issues of autonomy, cultural identity, and historical marginalization. The resistance to Indian state authority manifested not only in armed conflict but also in a broader societal discontent that was indicative of deeper systemic fractures within the region.

On November 14, 1978, the central government of India intervened by imposing President's rule in Manipur, a constitutional provision that dissolved the state government and entrusted governance to the Union Government. This move was ostensibly aimed at restoring order and addressing the escalating insurgent activities, which had been categorized as unlawful associations under the

Unlawful Activities (Prevention) Act of 1967. Notwithstanding these governmental measures, the persistence of extremist operations highlighted the limitations of the state's coercive apparatus in successfully managing the insurgency.

In a significant escalation of the security measures employed, Manipur was designated a "disturbed area" on September 8, 1980. This classification was predicated on the assessment that the ongoing insurgency and associated ethnic conflicts were of such magnitude that they severely disrupted public peace and order. The determination of "disturbed area" status is rooted in the interpretations of state governance, wherein any growth of conflict—whether of religious, racial, linguistic, or regional dimensions—can prompt such a designation. Following this classification, the Armed Forces Special Powers Act (AFSPA) of 1958 was implemented in Manipur, granting extraordinary powers to the armed forces to operate in "disturbed areas" with a mandate to restore order. The application of AFSPA consequently catalysed a paradigm of militarization that sought to quell dissent but often exacerbated resentment among the Manipuri. The local reaction to the imposition of AFSPA was marked by widespread protests and civil unrest, reflecting a significant collective objection to perceived state overreach and the resultant violations of civil liberties. Such socio-political upheaval illustrated the complexities of governance in regions grappling with insurgency, where security measures often clash with the fundamental rights and aspirations of the local people.

The veteran filmmaker Pabung Aribam recounts how ordinary people have suffered during that time, drawing from his own personal experiences. Pabung shares, "It was in 1976 when I received the National Film Award for Best Feature Film in Manipuri at the 24th National Film Awards for *Saaphabee* (1976). In the late 1970s, the area surrounding our home was lush with bamboo and trees. Back then, our neighbourhood in Imphal resembled a village more than an urban locality. There was a bamboo grove in the backyard of my house. One night, a group of Army men arrived at my house, their faces concealed by masks so I could not identify them. With a gun pointed at my head, they interrogated me, asking where I was hiding insurgents and why I was sheltering them in my home. Two officers questioned me in my drawing room, where my National Film Award for Saaphabee was prominently displayed. Upon noticing the award, they seemed to realize that I was a filmmaker. After some time, they left. The following morning, I reported the incident to the Superintendent of Police, who later informed me it was a routine check. It was one of the most harrowing experiences I faced during that period."

The transformation of Manipur into a "disturbed area" not only captured the state's efforts to regain control but also highlighted the intricate intricacies between insurgency, state authority, and civil resistance. The events of this period remain a poignant reminder of the challenges faced in administering peace in a context marked by deep-seated historical grievances and the quest for self-determination among diverse ethnic groups within the state. The legacy of these dynamics continues to shape the political discourse and social landscape in Manipur.

On July 11, 2004, the lifeless body of Thangjam Manorama Devi, a 29-year-old Manipuri woman, was discovered brutally assaulted near Ngariyan Mapao Maring Village, igniting widespread protests across India demanding justice and the repeal of the Armed Forces (Special Powers) Act of 1958 (AFSPA). This controversial law grants military and paramilitary forces extensive powers, leading to numerous human rights violations in Manipur. "The judicial inquiry report on the murder of Thangjam Manorama, a Manipuri girl, in 2004, handed over to the Supreme Court recently after being kept under wraps for over a decade, reveals the "brutal and merciless torture" by a 17 Assam Rifles team" (Rajagopal, 2021). An examination of the judicial inquiry report on the Thangjam Manorama case serves as a paradigmatic illustration of the rooted dynamics of violence and impunity that pervade conflict zones, particularly in Manipur governed by extraordinary security measures. The disclosure of the report after an inordinate period of ten years highlights the institutionalized mechanisms of confusion, cover-up, and delay that often characterize the response to extrajudicial killings and human rights abuses. The "brutal and merciless torture" inflicted upon Manorama, as described in the report by Rajagopal, is a stark testament to the systemic disregard for human life and dignity inherent to military occupation and state repression. The involvement of a team from the 17 Assam Rifles further highlights the complicity of state-sanctioned violence in facilitating the perpetuation of such abuses. This case highlights the significance of the "Arms Act" in Manipur, which has been used to justify the arbitrary detention, torture, and killing of civilians by security forces. The report's findings thus shed light on the instrumental role of legislation in shaping the modalities of state violence and perpetuating human rights violations. The delay in releasing the report and the subsequent handover to the Supreme Court raise critical questions about the value of institutional mechanisms in addressing human rights abuses. The report's disclosure after such an extended period emphasizes the need for more robust and independent oversight mechanisms to prevent impunity and ensure accountability for such crimes.

A critical examination of the Thangjam Manorama case also draws attention to the structural and historical antecedents of violence in Manipur. The ongoing insurgency, militarization, and state repression in the region have created a context in which human rights abuses are not only overlooked but also rooted, thereby perpetuating the cycles of violence and impunity.

People of Manipur came out to the street for the protest and the protests saw the emergence of notable acts of defiance, such as the "naked protest," where elderly Manipuri women stripped and marched to Kangla Fort, proclaiming "Indian Army Rape Us" while seeking an end to the AFSPA. On 15 July 2004, these 12 *imas* (mother) had disrobed in front of the historic Kangla Fort in the heart of Imphal — then the headquarters of the Assam Rifles — carrying banners with messages painted in red. "Indian Army Rape Us", read one. "Indian Army Take Our Flesh", said another. The women were protesting against the brutal killing of Manorama Thangjam, a 32-year-old woman who had been picked up by Assam Rifles personnel in suspicious circumstances four days prior (Sirur, 2021).

The women's choice to disrobe was a direct challenge to the authority of the Indian state and a powerful statement against gendered violence. The banners carried by the protestors, with phrases like "Indian Army Rape Us" and "Indian Army Take Our Flesh," highlighted their anger and despair over the brutal killing of Manorama Thangjam. Manorama, a 32-year-old woman, had been taken by Assam Rifles personnel under dubious circumstances just days before the protest, and her death sparked outrage and grief in the community. The inclusion of stark and provocative language on the banners illustrates the depth of their suffering and the urgency of their demands for justice. This event is emblematic of the broader struggles faced by women in conflict zones, where their bodies become battlegrounds in the struggle for political power and autonomy. The protest not only calls attention to the specific incident of Manorama's death but also serves as a broader indictment of the violence and impunity that characterize military operations in the region.

Irom Chanu Sharmila emerged as another prominent figure, becoming known for her indefinite hunger strike against the Malom Massacre, where 11 civilians were killed by security forces. The Frontline reported that on November 5, 2000, a frail young woman from Manipur quietly sat on a hunger strike at Malom, near the site where three days earlier 10 civilians were shot dead while waiting at a bus stand by Indian paramilitary forces. Irom Chanu Sharmila had resolved to fast until the draconian Armed Forces (Special Powers) Act, (AFSPA), was repealed by the Central government…Not only did Irom Sharmila become a symbol of non-violent resistance against the brute force of the establishment and armed forces, she also assumed the stature of an incorruptible, uncompromising martyr for the people of not just Manipur, but all the States where AFSPA was imposed (Frontline, 2022).

Again, in response to Manorama's death, Apunba Lup, an alliance of 32 organizations, called for the repeal of AFSPA. The state government established an inquiry commission led by C. Upendra Singh; however, the release of its findings was hindered by a court injunction. Chief Minister Okram

Ibobi Singh announced on August 12, 2004, that AFSPA would remain in effect in most areas of Manipur except for specific constituencies in Imphal.

The AFSPA and its impact on society has stirred a new wave of Manipuri filmmakers. Internationally known filmmaker, Haobam Paban Kumar made a documentary *AFSPA-1958* (2006) that investigates the protests following Manorama's death, capturing the unity of the Manipuri people against the draconian law. Similarly, another noted filmmaker Maibam Amarjeet Singh's documentary *City of Victims* (2009) addresses the troubling phenomenon of fake encounters and highlights two tragic murders by police forces in Imphal, challenging the narratives surrounding state-sponsored violence. Borun Thokchom's *The Silent Poet* (2011) explores the life of Irom Sharmila, who, while imprisoned, chronicles her thoughts in a notebook, shedding light on the poetic aspects of her long-standing protest. Furthermore, Saikhom Ratan's *Beyond Blast* (2021) delves into the socio-political landscape of Manipur, focusing on the experiences of civilians affected by ongoing violence, exemplified by artist Konthoujam Maikel Meitei, who uses his art to navigate his trauma after losing his legs in a bombing. Sonia Nepram's documentary *Bloody Phanek* (2017) addresses the cultural significance of the phanek, a traditional garment worn by Meitei women, using it as a symbol of protest while examining its connections to themes of purity and oppression. Her earlier film, *Gun and a God* (2013), presents the compelling story of Purnima, a Manipuri woman who turns to armed resistance after suffering injustices at the hands of the government.

Together, these documentaries reflect a broader movement against AFSPA and the fight for justice in Manipur. Supported by diverse groups including scholars, filmmakers, NGOs, and activists, this ongoing struggle highlights the urgent need for awareness and action against the violations of human rights and civil liberties prevalent in the region.

Ban on Hindi Films

In the cinematic space of Manipur, a disruption occurred as "in 2000, the insurgent group Revolutionary People's Front issued a notice banning Hindi, specifically Bollywood movies, for allegedly destroying Manipuri culture, language and local film industry. The outfit believed Bollywood went against Manipuri values. In due course, the militants confiscated thousands of video cassettes of Hindi films and music and burnt them as a mark of protest against the "Indianisation" of Manipur. The ban killed off the movie theatre circuit in the state…the last time a Hindi movie screened at a theatre hall in Manipur was *Kuch Kuch Hota Hai* in the late 1990s" (Bahn, 2023). The imposition of a ban on Hindi cinema in Manipur by the Revolutionary People's Front (RPF) in 2000 reflects a broader discourse on cultural preservation and identity in the face of globalization and external cultural influences. This ban resulted in the closure of numerous theaters, although the Assam Rifles responded by screening Hindi films at their cantonment. However, the ban represents an assertion of regional identity against the backdrop of a dominant national narrative often embodied by Hindi cinema. The last Hindi film screened in the state, *Kuch Kuch Hota Hai* (1998), symbolizes an era before the enforcement of the ban, marking a significant cultural shift in the region. This restriction on Hindi films is indicative of the tensions that arise when local cultures contend with influences from more established cultural industries.

In times of turmoil, when societal structures are challenged and traditional narratives are disrupted, filmmakers and artists serve as vital cultural agents who document, critique, and reinterpret the socio-political issues at hand. Filmmakers in Manipur, for instance, often utilize the medium of cinema not just as a form of entertainment but as a powerful tool for social commentary. By incorporating local dialects, folk narratives, and traditional storytelling techniques, these filmmakers preserve and promote the cultural nuances specific to Manipur Similarly, theater practitioners in Manipur contribute to this cultural dialogue through their plays, which may dramatize local histories and contemporary challenges faced by the community. Such legendary playwrights and directors of Manipur are Ratan Thiyam and Heisnam Kanhailal. Thiyam's play *Imphal Imphal* (1982) reflects the then students' unrest. His Manipur Trilogy is a comment on the prevailing unrest in the state and people's protest against the Armed Forces (Special Powers) Act." While Heisnam Kanhailal said, "Manipur, my home state gave me my theatre. The brutalised life ridden with so many conflicts, a life battered and deformed beyond recognition gave birth to my theatre. I thought the servitude we are living in was ours own, localised to a very small political and geographical space" (Kanhailal, n.d.). Pabung Aribam's contribution to Manipur theatre is immense which I discussed in the later part of this book. Dr. Aribam Uttam Sharma, son of Pabung Aribam, is currently serving as an Assistant Professor in the Department of Philosophy at North-Eastern Hill University, Shillong, Meghalaya. He shares the following anecdote with the author: "I had the good fortune of having lunch with Oja Kanhailal and Ima Sabitri at Kalakshetra, a year before Oja passed away. During our conversation, he said something remarkable: 'We owe your father a great deal. Without him, we would not have come so far in theatre.' I found this surprising, as very few established theatre directors have made such acknowledgments publicly—except for the playwright Sri Biren, who once said on camera that without the efforts and contributions of Aribam, any history of Manipuri theatre would remain incomplete."

Manipuri Cinema: Where Tradition Meets Screen Magic!

Manipuri cinema is celebrated for its rich and varied legacy, tracing its roots back to the latter part of the twentieth century. The journey began with *Mainu Pemcha* (1948), inspired by the works of renowned Manipuri playwright Ayekpam Shyamsunder Singh and directed by Rathin Sen. A group of passionate cinephiles endeavoured to make the region's first film, but the film was ultimately left unfinished due to financial constraints. The narrative focused on the tragic tale of a young girl, Mainu Pemcha, who takes her own life following a misunderstanding with her lover. It poignantly explores the Meitei community's refusal to conduct farewell rites for her unnatural demise, leading to her body being discarded in an uninhabited place for stray animals. Veteran filmmaker Aribam Syam Sharma remarked, "I was fortunate to watch the rough cut (9 reels of the film) showcased at Imphal Talkies. Although the film was never completed, its profound impact on emerging Manipuri filmmakers is undeniable, inspiring them to pursue their cinematic dreams" (personal communication, April 30, 2021).

The 1970s marked a pivotal era for Manipuri cinema with the release of *Matamgi Manipur* (Contemporary Manipur, 1972), directed by Bengali filmmaker Deb Kumar Bose. Premiering on April 9, 1972, this film achieved a historic milestone by winning the President's Medal at the 20th National Film Festival. Matamgi Manipur, produced by Karam Monomohan under the banner of K.T. Films Private Limited, delves into themes of familial conflict and relationships. The story centers on a retired Amin who diligently saves money with the aspiration of visiting

Vrindaban, a revered pilgrimage site. However, as time progresses, the once-happy family—comprising his devoted wife, Tampak, their two sons, Ibohal and Ibotombi, and their daughter, Tondonbi—begins to unravel. The film poignantly addresses the erosion of familial values in the face of individual desires, ultimately concluding with a scene of reconciliation among the family members.

Sapam Nadia Chand, known as S.N. Chand, directed the landmark film *Brojendragee Luhongba* (Marriage of Brojendra), released on December 30, 1972. This film is pivotal in Manipuri culture and cinema, telling the poignant story of Brojendra, a young man studying at Calcutta Medical College. Despite his objections, his family arranges his marriage, echoing traditional customs. Initially indifferent to his wife, Brojendra's perspective shifts during a moonlit concert where he becomes captivated by a woman; unexpectedly, upon seeking to apologize to his wife, he discovers she is the woman he admires. Chand's second film, *Ngak-e-ko Nangse* (How Surprising a Person You Are, 1974), explores themes of love and rejection through the lives of two young women, Shanti and Anita. Shanti, sold by her aunt after her parents' death, finds solace and love with Binoy, though struggles with his mother's cruel behaviour and ultimately leaves him to give birth alone. Meanwhile, Anita faces rejection from her boyfriend, Ravi, after becoming pregnant. Despite their hardships, both narratives converge towards a hopeful conclusion.

The film society movement in Manipur flourished in the mid-1960s, marked by the establishment of the Film Society of Manipur in 1966, with Hijam Romani Singh and Nongmaithem Sharat at the helm as President and Secretary. It was a pivotal moment in the region's cultural landscape, leading to the society's registration under the Federation of Film Societies of India in 1969. Within this vibrant atmosphere, a passionate dreamer named M.A. Singh yearned to immerse himself in the world of cinema. His aspiration took flight as he sought admission to India's renowned Film and Television Institute of India (FTII) in Pune, where he enrolled in 1969. At FTII, Singh carved a unique path, becoming the first Manipuri to study there. He received diplomas in both editing and direction, furthering his journey into the artistic realm. Notably, he was also the first Manipuri to make films in Hindi as part of his studies, showcasing his pioneering spirit. During his time at FTII, he directed two diploma films that captured the essence of human experiences. His first work, *Maan Apman* (Respect-Humiliation, 1973), is a poignant 19-minute narrative that follows a young man who anxiously awaits the return of a long-lost friend. The friend, who arrives in the city seeking medical help, finds himself unable to secure a doctor. Promising to assist, the young man encourages his friend to return the next day. However, when the dawn breaks, he is met with tragedy—their reunion is cut short by the death of his friend, who fails to recognize him in his final moments. Singh's second film, *Citizen* (1973), is an introspective 11-minute exploration of individual responsibility toward one's country, delving into the moral obligations that bind citizens to their society. Upon returning to Manipur, M.A. Singh was determined to breathe new life into Manipuri cinema. In an environment where professional producers were nearly non-existent, he began producing documentaries for various government and non-government projects, using his skills to tell stories that mattered. Despite the challenges, he persevered and, after an almost eight-year wait, he finally realized his dream of making a Manipuri feature film with *Sanakeithel* (Golden Market, 1983). This groundbreaking film garnered critical acclaim, winning the Rajat Kamal award for Best Regional Film at the 31st National Film Festival in 1984. Sanakeithel, narrated through the eyes of a young boy named Ibungobi, affectionately known as Mobi, unfolds a harrowing yet deeply human story. It portrays the aftermath of his widowed mother, Nungshi, suffering a horrific gang rape in their village, capturing the ensuing chaos—her descent into madness, her subsequent disappearance, and the harsh treatment Mobi experiences at the hands of his maternal relatives. The film is a poignant exploration of loss, innocence, and the search for maternal love, shedding light on the intersection of personal tragedy and societal neglect. The film Sanakeithel paved the way for future generations of filmmakers.

The 1980s emerged as a pivotal decade for Manipuri cinema, often regarded as its Golden Era, despite the prevailing socio-political turmoil catalysed by the Armed Forces (Special Powers) Act of 1958 (AFSPA) and significant upheaval in the region. This flourishing era can be attributed to a confluence of factors that encapsulated both institutional development and creative renaissance within the filmmaking community of Manipur. A significant advancement in this course was the establishment of the Manipur State Film Development Council in 1980, that reflects the collective efforts of young filmmakers, cinephiles, intellectuals, and writers dedicated to nurturing the region's cultural identity. This institution, which later evolved into the Manipur Film Development Corporation in 1987, functioned under the aegis of the Art and Culture Department. Its primary mission was to facilitate the growth of Manipuri cinema through financial assistance to emerging filmmakers.

The year 1984 marked another major milestone with the initiation of the first Manipur State Film Festival, an event designed to incentivize and honour the technicians, filmmakers, and all contributors to the cinematic arts in the region.

The decade was further distinguished by the remarkable accomplishments of the acclaimed filmmaker Aribam Syam Sharma, whose seminal film *Imagi Ningthem* (My Son, My Precious, 1981) drove Manipuri cinema onto the global stage. The film garnered the Grand Prix at the Festival of Three Continents in Nantes, France, in 1982, marking a historic recognition as the first Manipuri film to achieve international acclaim. The awards received at the 29th National Film Awards, including the Rajat Kamal and recognition for Best Child Artist (Master Leikhendra), signified not only the artistic merit of the film but also its influential role in portraying Manipuri culture and social realities to a broader audience. In addition to narrative cinema, documentary filmmaking also prospered during this decade, exemplified by Aribam's documentary *Sangai– The Dancing Deer of Manipur* (1988). This documentary, produced by the Sangeet Natak Akademi, illustrated the rich cultural heritage of Manipur through the portrayal of the ballet "Keibul Lamjao". Honored as the Outstanding Film of the Year 1989 by the British Film Institute in London, the documentary highlighted the intricate relationship between art and the natural landscape of the region.

In the 1980s, a group of Manipuri filmmakers made significant contributions to the film history. Some notable examples include *Wangma Wangma* (Opposite Sides) by Laimayum Bankabihari Sharma in 1981 and *Yairipok Thambalnu* (A Girl from Yairipok) in 1984. K. Ibohal Sharma's Thaba (1984), Th. Dorendra's works such as *Sanakhya Ebotombi*, *Eche Sakhi* (Elder Sister Sakhi in 1986) and G. Narayan Sharma's *Kombirei* (Kombirei flower in 1989) are also worth mentioning. However, it was Aribam Syam Sharma who first made a lasting impact on the Manipuri film narrative, followed by M.A. Singh. Singh's second feature film, was *Langlen Thadoi* (1984).

Shot entirely in full colour, the film, *Langlen Thadoi* was the "first feature-length film" in Manipur to be made in colour in 1984. However, Pabung's *Paokhum Ama* (1983), a 54-minute film, was made in colour prior to *Langlen Thadoi.* Additionally, *Langlen Thadoi* was the first Manipuri film to be produced by a woman, Kh. Sakhi Devi, under the Kay Pee Films International banner. *Langlen Thadoi's* story revolves around a young girl named Thadoi, who, after her parents' and then her aunt Leihao's death, decides to dedicate her life to making a positive impact on society.

The late 1960s and 1970s marked the advent of the film society movement in India, which significantly transformed thc landscape of Manipuri cinema. A notable milestone was the establishment of the Imphal Cine Club in 1979 by visionaries Aribam Syam Sharma, R.K. Bidur, and K. Ibohal. This initiative played a crucial role in introducing international films to the local audience, creating a bridge between global cinema and the people of Manipur. The subsequent organization of the Manipur State Film Festival in the 1980s further enriched this cultural dialogue. This era ignited a newfound awareness of the significance of filmmaking in shaping cultural narratives and societal reflections.

The 1990s heralded yet another transformative phase for Manipuri cinema. Under the footstep of Aribam Syam Sharma, a group of innovative filmmakers began to emerge, who, having been influenced by various artistic disciplines, sought to challenge the conventions of traditional filmmaking. Their work shunned mere commercial storytelling in favour of tackling socially relevant issues, reflecting the turbulent context of the insurgency that was gripping Manipur during that period. This led to films that were not only aesthetically engaging but also deeply resonant with the socio-political realities of their time. One of the defining achievements of Manipuri cinema in the 1990s was the international recognition gained by Aribam's landmark film, *Ishanou* (The Chosen One, 1990). Selected for the prestigious Un Certain Regard category at the 44th Cannes Film Festival, the film stood out as an artistic exploration of the Maibi, a cultural belief rooted in Manipuri society, and introduced audiences both in India and abroad to this hitherto unfamiliar phenomenon. The film's recognition did not stop at Cannes; it garnered significant accolades, including the Rajat Kamal for Best Regional Film at the 38th National Film Festival in 1991, where Anoubam Kiranmala was also honored with a Special Mention for her compelling performance as the lead actress.

A new wave of filmmakers, including Oken Amakcham, emerged in Manipuri cinema, blending popular styles with meaningful storytelling. Amakcham debuted with *Khonthang* (Sound Wave, 1992), which was showcased in the Indian Panorama at IFFI 1993. The film follows a destitute family relying on their younger brother for salvation, only to find he returns with a girl from a wealthy family, choosing to live with her instead. His second film, *Mayophygee Macha* (The Son of Mayophy), won the Rajat Kamal at the 42nd National Film Awards in 1994. It tells the story of a single mother who raises her son to become a successful athlete, highlighting the struggles single mothers face in society. In *Aroiba Bidai* (The Last Goodbye, 1999), Amakcham addresses the contemporary social issues in Manipur, including insurgency, through the story of Tamphajao, who gets arrested for sheltering insurgents and goes missing. He also made *Lanmei* (Wildfire, 2002), marking him as the first Manipuri filmmaker to have a digital film commercially released.

Producer-turned-director Konhbrailatpam Ibohal Sharma emerged as a key figure in the new wave of Manipuri cinema with his film *Sambal Wangma* (The Other Side of the Fence, 1993), which won the Rajat Kamal for Best Regional Film. The story revolves around Joy and Ibeni, cousins in Meitei society whose love leads them to elope, challenging conservative norms that forbid their union and highlighting the struggle between tradition and personal choice. Filmmaker Makhonmani Mongsaba made his mark with *Chatledo Eidee* (Gone I Am, 2000), an intense love story about Shandhyarani and Shailesh, thwarted by poverty. Shandhyarani marries someone else, leaving Shailesh heartbroken, thus exploring the tragic impact of societal and economic pressures on love. The film received the Rajat Kamal at the 48th National Film Awards and was featured in the Indian Panorama at the 32nd International Film Festival of

India. In *Yenning Amadi Likla* (Spring and Dew, 2007), Mongsaba delves into the emotional turmoil experienced by a boy named Sanatomba amid parental conflicts. Using the metaphor of a bird and a kite, he illustrates Sanatomba's desire for escape. The film concludes with hope as a childless couple offers to adopt him, despite his family's challenges. It was screened in the Indian Panorama at the 39th International Film Festival of India. In *Nangna Kappa Pakchade* (Tears of a Woman, 2013), Mongsaba tells the story of Nungshithoi, a Manipuri woman abandoned by her lover during pregnancy. The narrative follows a young lawyer who advocates for justice on her behalf, shedding light on the plight of women in society.

Cinematographer-turned-director Laimayum Surjakanta Sharma's film *Meiree* (The Flame, 1999) paints a socio-political portrait of Manipur, highlighting the corrupt nexus between police and politicians, alongside the emergence of rebel groups aiming to combat it. His follow-up film, *Hayengna Kanagee* (Who's Turn is Tomorrow? 2000), delves into societal decay as a corrupt alliance of a politician, a police officer, and criminals deceive the public. The protagonist, Meiraba, rallies his friends to challenge the gang, but the majority fall victim, leaving only Premi. Ultimately, she seeks revenge against the corrupt and discards her weapons, emphasizing that peace cannot be sustainably achieved through violence. *Zehra* (1999), directed by Chandam Shyamacharan and Chandam Manorama, tells the story of a young Pangal woman who defies her community's restrictive customs. Her admiration for Meitei culture isolates her and her mother, who faces ostracism due to her romance with a Meitei man amidst ongoing ethnic tensions.

Laimayum Bankabihari Sharma founded the "Film Chamber" in 1976 to nurture emerging filmmakers. His notable works include *Madhabee* (1993), *Meichak* (Feeling of Hurt, 2000), and *Poppy* (2000), each tackling complex themes. Meichak follows Dwijen's journey of coping with love lost, while Poppy addresses the conflict between a drug dealer and an honest officer battling the drug trade, culminating in violence as familial bonds strain under pressure.

The 1990s ushered in a wave of talented filmmakers, including R.K. Kripa, Chand Heisnam, Khwairakpam Bishwamittra and others, driving Manipuri cinema to new heights of artistic expression.

Despite such ethnic tensions and unrest in the 1990s and 2000s, filmmakers like Haobam Paban Kumar emerged, used cinema as a powerful medium to express marginalized narratives. Paban's notable works *Nine Hills One Valley*, which confronts the issue of ethnic violence through personal stories and his most recent film, *Joseph's Son*, examines shared humanity amidst community differences. Paban's films have garnered international recognition, showcasing his distinctive storytelling approach that resonates with local contexts while addressing broader themes of conflict and compassion. In addition to these significant projects, Paban's other noteworthy films in his oeuvre include *Ngaihak Lambida* (Along the Way, 2006), *A Cry in the Dark* (2006), *The First Leap* (2016), *Mr. India* (2009), *Nupishabi* (Women Impersonate, 2010), and *Phum Shang* (Floating Life, 2014). His documentary *Pabung Syam* (Father Syam, 2021) continues to reflect his dedication to exploring the rich and complex narratives of Manipur.

A new wave of filmmakers, including Haorongbam Maipaksana Singh, is driving the evolution of Manipuri cinema by tackling local issues through both feature films and documentaries. Maipaksana, who holds a diploma in editing from the Dr. Bhupen Hazarika Regional Government Film & Television Institute, made *Eibushu Yaohanbiyu* (2015), a story about a differently-abled boy named Khelemba who defies social prejudice to pursue his passion for football, ultimately leading his team to victory. This film won the Best Manipuri Feature Film at the 63rd National Film Awards. His subsequent work, *Wonnam* (Scent of a Flower), highlights themes of unity among diverse ethnic communities through the story of Leihao, an orthodox Hindu Meitei who marries a Christian Tangkhul and endeavors to foster peace among her communities. Another film, *Phijigee Mani* (My Only Gem, 2011), deals with the complexities of a mother-son relationship amid socio-political challenges in Manipur.

Bobby Wahengbam has also made notable contributions, co-directing *Eigi Kona* (Stallone, My Pony, 2019), which explores the struggles of polo players, and *Apaiba Leichil* (Floating Clouds, 2021), addressing societal challenges faced by the third gender. Filmmakers like Oinam Gautam Singh have made films such as *Eidee Kadaida* (Where Am I, 2014) and *Pandam Amada* (In Pursuit of, 2019), with Phijigee Mani earning national recognition. Romi Meitei's *Eikhoigi Yum* (Our Home, 2021) examines globalization's impact on a lakeside fishing community. Oinam Doren has distinguished himself through relevant documentaries like *Songs of Mashangva* (2010) and *Frozen in Fear* (2022), while Meena Longjam focuses on female narratives in her impactful documentaries, winning the National Award for *Auto Driver* (2015) and *Achoubi in Love* (2018). Her documentary *Andro Dreams* (2023) was the opening film in the Indian Panorama Non-Feature Film section at the 54th International Film Festival of India (2023) and also got selected for the official selection at the 15th International Documentary and Short Film Festival of Kerala 2023. *Andro Dreams* tells a touching story about resilience and empowerment through Phanjoubam Laibi, an elderly woman with a strong spirit living in a traditional village in Northeast India. As the leader of a girls' football club that has existed for over thirty years, Laibi represents the struggles and dreams of women in a male-dominated society. The club is not just about sports; it challenges the unfair treatment of women. The film highlights the difficulties women face, especially in rural areas while celebrating the importance of friendship and teamwork among women as they support each other through tough times.

Another Manipuri film that has garnered international acclaim is *Boong* (2024) directed by Lakshmipriya Devi, which had its world premiere in the Discovery section of the 49th Toronto International Film Festival (TIFF). The film as a cinematic adaptation of her grandmother's stories, drawing inspiration from the folk tales shared during Manipur's turbulent period in the late 1970s and early 1980s. The narrative focuses on Boong, a young student contending with the complexities of racial tensions and border issues in Manipur, as he is driven by an unwavering determination to reunite his fractured family.

Manipuri cinema takes pride in having three jury members selected for the prestigious 55th International Film Festival of India (IFFI 2024). Filmmaker Borun Thokchom is on the International Cinema committee, while filmmaker Ronel Haobam serves on the jury for the Non-Feature Film section of the Indian Panorama. Oinam Gautam is a jury for the Feature Film section at the Indian Panorama.

Pioneers like Gurumayum Narayan Sharma and M.K. Binodini have helped build the foundation of Manipuri cinema, inspiring new filmmakers. G. Narayan Sharma (1922 – 2007), started his career as a photographer but was also passionate about music, dance, and acting. He danced with the Little Ballet Troupe in Bombay for six years and toured with the Triveni Kala Sangam ballet group. He got into films when he met famous actor Balraj Sahni, which inspired him to explore acting and cinematography. He produced Manipur's first film to run for 100 days, *Lamja Pashuram* (1974), *Saaphabee* (1976), and *Helloy* (2002), leaving a significant legacy in Manipuri cinema. Maharaj Kumari Binodini Devi (1922–2011) was a notable literary figure from Manipur, whose contributions to literature and the arts have garnered her significant acclaim. In the later stages of her life, she authored a collection of essays that tenderly reflect upon her experiences growing up as a princess in the regal confines of her palace. Binodini's prolific oeuvre includes novels, short stories, essays, plays, award-winning screenplays, as well as compositions for melodies and ballet, which collectively have facilitated her recognition on a global scale. In 1976, she was honoured with the Padma Shri award in acknowledgement of her literary accomplishments. In 1979, she received the Sahitya Akademi Award for her 1976 historical novel, *Boro Saheb Ongbi Sanatombi*. Binodini's work in films and literature still influences Manipuri cinema today. Critics such as the late R.K. Bidur, Meghachandra Kongbam, and Bobby Wahengbam have worked to improve discussions about Manipuri cinema, helping us understand its history and promote its achievements across the country.

A Multilingual Cinematic Renaissance in Manipur

Manipur is a linguistically rich region where various ethnic languages coexist alongside the Meitei language. Aribam Syam Sharma says that in Manipur, there are more than 40 different dialects, and now everyone wants to have their own identity, their own language, and their own education. I think this is important because once a language is lost, it is lost forever. It is also important to have these cultures and identities that are distinct, or in one way exclusive, but at the same time inclusive. This is the way we havc to live now in the world. Culturally we may have differences, but we must respect each other and each culture so that society can be inclusive (Enzmann, 2019). The linguistic diversity of Manipur, characterized by the existence of over 40 distinct dialects, serves as a salient example of the intricate interaction between identity, language, and education in a culturally rich society. Aribam's assertion that "everyone wants to have their own identity, their own language, and their own education" reflects a broader global trend towards the affirmation of individual and community identities in the face of globalization. Language is not only a medium of communication but also a vessel of culture, tradition, and collective memory; thus, the preservation of dialects becomes paramount. His observation that "once a language is lost, it is lost forever" emphasises the key value of linguistic heritage, highlighting the irreversible nature of language death and its implications for cultural continuity. The duality of distinctiveness and inclusivity that emerges from language preservation is a crucial aspect of contemporary sociocultural dynamics. Aribam's argument advocates for respect and recognition among diverse cultures, positing that such an ethos is essential for societal inclusivity. This respect is vital in justifying ethnocentrism and xenophobia, inspiring intercultural dialogue. He fosters a pluralistic society where multiple identities coexist harmoniously.

In the 2010s, a new generation of filmmakers began making films in their local dialects, Notable among these is Ashok Veilou, the first tribal filmmaker from the Poumai Naga tribe to earn a Master's in Direction and Screenplay Writing from the Satyajit Ray Cinema & Television Institute. Veilou's short films, *Tou-Tai* (2016) and *Look at the Sky* (2017), both in Poula language, received acclaim, with Tou-Tai winning the Golden Royal Bengal Tiger at the 2018 Kolkata International Film Festival. This film follows a young insurgent grappling with his identity amid socio-political turmoil in Manipur.

Veilou's brother, Alexander Leo Pou, directed the heartfelt documentary *My Grandpa's Home* (2012) and the film *Pony Tale* (2018), highlighting the Ponies of Manipur. Similarly, Sng. Pearson Anal from the Anal tribe made *Peral Thingbo* (Tree of Secrets, 2023), a film in the Anal dialect that tells the transformative story of Momo, who encounters the beautiful Khikhi. This film won multiple awards at the 2023 Tribal Film Festival in Manipur. Directors Boris Golmei and Pilot Kamei, from the Rongmei tribe, made the film *Siang* (The Curse, 2023), which explores themes of bravery and friendship through a story of five friends defending their land.

The Tangkhul community has also made its mark with films like *Huinaya Phaningkakhui* (Too Late to Realize, 1986) being the first Tangkhul film. The Tangkhul Naga Film Association (TNFA), founded in 1985, has since supported local filmmakers, leading to the production of around one hundred films. A young filmmaker, A. C. Rinshing, debuted with *Samkhok* (Morung Bed, 2023), exploring pre-Christian customs and family dynamics in the Tangkhul community. Another Tangkhul film, *Zingthanwo* (Morning Star, 2023), co-directed by Makanmi Ramror and Seema Ks Awungshi, portrays a love story complicated by class conflicts. The TNFA further advanced Tangkhul cinema by hosting the Tangkhul Naga Film Festival 2023 in Ukhrul Town, marking a significant milestone in the region's cinematic history.

The recent wave of ethnic conflict between the Meitei community and the Kuki tribes that erupted on May 3, 2023, has disrupted this intricate social fabric. The violence associated with this strife has drawn significant attention from both domestic and international media, casting a spotlight on the socio-political dynamics of the region and raising questions about identity, belonging, and coexistence. In the face of such adversity, various cultural organizations have endeavoured to use art, particularly cinema, as a vehicle for reconciliation and understanding, culminating in initiatives such as the North East India Film Festival (NEIFF). This lens of cinema reveals not only the struggles of the communities but also the immense potential for dialogue, expression, and ultimately, healing.

The ethnic conflict in Manipur has its roots in historical grievances and socio-political dynamics that have long characterized the region. Since India's independence, issues of identity and representation have often led to tensions between various ethnic groups. The Meiteis, who predominantly reside in the Imphal Valley, have historically held significant political and economic power, while the Kukis and other tribal communities, largely found in the hill districts, have sought to assert their voices and rights. As the conflict escalated, it became evident that underlying tensions regarding land, resources, and identity were exacerbating the situation, leading to a violent outpouring that shocked the region. Given the seriousness of this situation, the initiatives taken by THOUNA Manipur, Film Forum Manipur, and dedicated art and culture enthusiasts have underscored the belief that cinema can transcend these divides. Organized with the support of the Union Information and Broadcasting Ministry, the NEIFF took place from March 3 to 7, 2024, providing a crucial platform for filmmakers from the eight North-Eastern states of

India. The significance of the festival lies not merely in its execution but in its potential as a cultural intervention aimed at fostering dialogue, understanding, and ultimately, peace.

Again, on February 12, 2025, the second North East India Film Festival (NEIFF) was officially inaugurated at the City Convention Centre in Imphal, capital city of Manipur. This five-day event served as a platform to highlight the region's rich and diverse film heritage, which has been gaining recognition globally. The festival was organized by THOUNA, Manipur, in collaboration with Film Forum Manipur and the Directorate of Information and Public Relations (DIPR) from the Government of Manipur. The event also received significant support from the Ministry of Information and Broadcasting of the Indian Government and the National Film Development Corporation (NFDC). Throughout the festival, a total of 28 films were showcased, including eight feature films and two short films selected for the competition section. This diverse line-up catered to the varying tastes of the audience, providing a glimpse into the creative world of film-making from the region.

With the establishment of the Manipur State Film and Television Institute in 2016, the institute has acted as a catalyst, empowering local filmmakers to create content that echoes with their lived experiences. The celebration of the Golden Jubilee of Manipuri cinema in 2021 is indicative of the cinema's evolution.

Within this vibrant cinematic landscape, Sanju Bachaspatimayum stands out as a prominent figure. As the secretary of the Manipur State Film Development Society (MSFDS) and a noted filmmaker, he has significantly influenced the course of Manipuri cinema. His commitment to mentoring young filmmakers and creating an inclusive environment has led to the emergence of a new wave of cinematic voices.

The importance of language in cinema cannot be overstated, especially in a region like Manipur, where multiple dialects and languages coalesce. The NEIFF's dedication to films in Meitei, Tangkhul, Poula, and other tribal dialects highlights the festival's commitment to inclusivity. Each language serves as a vessel of culture, history, and identity; as such, the portrayal of these diverse narratives is crucial not only for cultural preservation but also for facilitating dialogue across communities.

To fully appreciate the course of cinema in Manipur, one must delve into the region's complex history and cultural legacy.

***

Works Cited

Bahn, D. (2023, August 16). Tribals defy ban, screen Hindi movies in Manipur after 23 years. The New Indian Express. https://www.newindianexpress.com/nation/2023/Aug/16/tribals-defy-ban-screen-hindi-movies-in-manipur-after-23-years-2605771.

Chisthi, S. M. A. W. (2005). *Political development in Manipur (1919-1949).* Kalpaz Publications.

Enzmann, J. (2019). Interview with three leading documentary filmmakers from Northeast India: Aribam Syam Sharma, Haobam Paban Kumar, and Pinky Brahma Choudhury. SPF Now. https://www.spf.org/en/publications/spfnow/0063.html

Frontline, T. (2022, August 20). 2000: Irom Sharmila begins fast for repeal of AFSPA. Frontline. https://frontline.thehindu.com/the-nation/india-at-75-epochal-moments-2000-irom-sharmila-begins-fast-for-repeal-of-afspa/article65720016.

Government of Manipur. (n.d.). *Annexure-1: Comprehensive details about Manipur State and its environmental & social sensitivities.* Retrieved from https://manipur.gov.in/wp-content/uploads/2015/03/annexure-01-manipur-comprehensive.pdf.

Furber, H. (1951), "The Unification of India, 1947–1951", *Pacific Affairs*, 24 (4), Pacific Affairs, University of British Columbia: 352–371, doi:10.2307/2753451, JSTOR 2753451

Kanhailal, H. (n.d). TODAY in Today theatre: Part 1. e-pao. Retrieved January 30, 2022, from https://www.epao.net/epSubPageExtractor.asp?src=manipur.Shumang_Lila.TODAY_in_today_theatre_Part_1_By_H_Kanhailal

Maibam Chanu, B. (2022, January 10). *The seven years' devastation (1819-1826) in Manipur. News From Manipur - Imphal Times.* https://www.imphaltimes.com/guest-column/the-seven-years-devastation-1819-1826-in-manipur/

Mutuwa, M. B. (2019). COLONIALISM AND THE PRINCELY STATE OF MANIPUR. *Proceedings of the Indian History Congress*, *79*, 448–456. https://www.jstor.org/stable/26906278

Pathou, W. "Biography of His Highness Maharaja Bodhachandra (Last King of Manipur) - Part 3." *The Sangai Express*, 5 Dec. 2013.

Rajagopal, K. (2021, November 17). Manorama 'mercilessly tortured.' The Hindu. https://www.thehindu.com/news/national/Manorama-death-brutal-torture-probe-panel/article60440983.

Sirur, S., (2021, July 22). 17 years since their naked protest against Army, 'Mothers of Manipur' say fight not over yet. The Print. https://theprint.in/india/17-years-since-their-naked-protest-against-army-mothers-of-manipur-say-fight-not-over-yet/700093/

Chapter Two

From Dreams to Reality: The Aribam Saga Begins

Indian cinema is a mix of many different stories from various regions. Among these voices, Manipuri cinema is unique and interesting, known for its stories and its strong connection to Manipuri culture. At the helm of this artistic evolution stands Pabung Aribam, a cinematic maestro who took Manipuri cinema on the global map. Born in the mid 1930s amidst the lush landscapes of Manipur, Aribam Syam Sharma's formative years were steeped in the vibrant traditions of his homeland, Manipur. This region, famous for its exquisite classical dance forms, melodious music, and rich folklore, provided him with an artistic foundation. From an early age, the rhythms of Manipuri dance and the narratives of local dance form around him, inspiring a deep feel for storytelling that would evolve into a lifelong passion for filmmaking.

Pabung Aribam grew up in a place (Manipur) with many different ethnic groups and a complicated history. This environment gave him lots of ideas and inspiration for his art. In Pabung Aribam's cinematic world, storytelling becomes a vehicle for social commentary and cultural preservation. His films often traverse the delicate line between reality and myth, blending traditional narratives with contemporary issues. Whether they are made-up stories or real-life documentaries, his films let the world see how beautiful, and strong Manipuri culture is. They remind us that we all share similar stories, no matter where we come from.

Aribam Shyamkrishna Sharma was born on Saturday, March 21, 1936, in Thangmeiband Lourung Purel Leikai, situated in the vibrant and culturally rich region of Sana Phandeng Leirak, Imphal. He was raised in a family environment as the son of Aribam Kalachand Sharma and Aribam Ongbi Kongbrailatpam Borkanya Devi. After successfully completing the Indian School Certificate (ISC), Pabung Aribam enrolled at Visva-Bharati University, a prestigious institution renowned for its emphasis on liberal arts and culture. He pursued a Bachelor of Arts degree, which he obtained in 1956. His time at Visva-Bharati was pivotal, allowing him to immerse himself in the rich intellectual environment fostered by luminaries such as Rabindranath Tagore. It subsequently inspired him to continue his studies in philosophy. Committed to deepening his understanding of philosophical concepts and frameworks, Pabung Aribam broadened his academic pursuits and got a Master of Arts in Philosophy.

I have long been fascinated by the films of Aribam Syam Sharma, and when I had the chance to visit Imphal, Manipur, again in 2021, I didn't want to miss the opportunity to sit down with him and ask about his incredible journey as a filmmaker. I have always been drawn to his unique perspective and the rich thematic depth that infuses his films, and I was eager to learn more about the person behind the camera. As we settled into a lengthy conversation, I could not help but wonder why, despite his impressive body of work, Aribam's contributions often remain overlooked. During our conversation, he revealed the passions and influences that have shaped his artistic vision. It turned out that his first love was not cinema at all, but music, and it was through music that he developed an artistic expression that would eventually lead him to filmmaking.

Pabung Aribam was a reticent person, and I was not certain if he would be receptive to a lengthy conversation. To build rapport, I decided to sit down with him and ask my queries in a more informal manner, planning to pause and ask follow-up questions after brief intervals. To ensure that I could ask every aspect of our discussion, I requested filmmaker Monjul Baruah to record our conversation using my video camera. I also carried a backup voice recorder as a precautionary measure. As I prepared, Pabung Aribam leaned back in his chair, a distant expression in his eyes, and began to share a poignant story that had left an indelible mark on his childhood.

"My early years were overshadowed by the dark clouds of war. In 1942, during the initial wave of Japanese bombings on Imphal, my family was plunged into chaos. It was an ordinary Sunday, May 10, 1942, a day like any other, when I was just a curious six-year-old. I remember playing outside, the sun shining brightly, and laughter filling the air. But then, everything changed, there was this strange humming sound, not unlike a mosquito buzzing around your ear. It piqued my curiosity, and before I knew it, I was standing in the courtyard, my little heart racing. I looked up, and what I saw still feels surreal; a shimmering silver object was gliding through the clouds, as if it belonged to a dream. But in an instant, that enchanting sight turned into a nightmare. Suddenly, it burst apart, raining down chaos from the sky. Bombs fell like angry raindrops, and the world erupted in a cacophony of machine-gun fire, artillery blasts, and the chilling wails of emergency sirens. It was a moment that shattered not just the afternoon's tranquility but my childhood innocence as well."

Pabung continued that despite the warnings issued by British authorities, Pabung Aribam's family and his community found themselves unprepared for the subsequent mayhem. To protect themselves, they ingeniously constructed basic bomb shelters beneath their beds and practised drills to assist with their escape. The backyard had bamboo trees all around it. Someone had dug big holes in the shapes of letters, hoping they would be extra shelters. But these holes didn't help when things fell apart. People panicked and ran everywhere to find safety. Some barely avoided bombs that destroyed areas near their shelters. Others died in the trenches where they were hiding. Even though everything was ruined, there was a little bit of hope. Rainwater collected in the bomb craters, giving people water to drink when they didn't have enough food.

Pabung paused for a moment, his weary eyes reflecting the weight of his memories, and finally spoke, "You know, as I'm getting older, I find myself needing more rest. I can't keep talking endlessly." I nodded, giving him the space he needed. Slowly, he began to recount his experiences. He described to me how his family lived in close proximity to the cantonment area and the Burma Oil Company depot, a location that unfortunately became a prime target when the war began. The relentless bombings by the Japanese forces cast a dark shadow over their once bustling neighbourhood, turning it into a scene of chaos and despair. One particular haunting memory lingered vividly in his mind: a neighbour stumbling to their door, bloodied and bearing the jagged scars of splinter wounds. It was a sight that would haunt him for years. As he spoke, I could almost feel the heavy feeling of fear and sadness that covered the community. The sound of explosions disrupted daily life, surprising shoppers and causing total panic. He told a sad story about a bomb exploding during a prayer meeting, killing people who had gathered to pray. The weight of his words stayed in the air, reminding everyone how easily life can be taken away.

Pabung said that his father, a well-educated man who studied Sanskrit, was the chief astrologer for

Maharaj Bodhachandra of Manipur. He received the titles Panji Shanglakpa and Vidya Ratna. His father greatly loved the performing arts, especially Shumang Lila, a traditional play form based on stories from the Mahabharata, showing his strong connection to his culture. Among the children, Aribam was known to be the most devout. Aribam was deeply affected by his father's death when he was very young. Vivid images of funeral pyres along the riverbanks, with smoke rising sadly into the sky, suggested the tragic realities of that time.

Pabung Aribam's father passed away due to a cholera outbreak that occurred during the Second World War. This outbreak formed part of a larger pandemic that impacted much of Southeast Asia. Richard Flanagan's *The Narrow Road to the Deep North* describes the historical context of this period, noting that in 1942, following the Japanese conquest of Burma from the British, the Japanese sought to use Burma as a base for launching an attack on India. Because Allied forces were bombing sea routes, the Japanese began constructing a railway from Bangkok (in what is now Thailand) to Rangoon (now Yangon) in Burma (now Myanmar), using forced labor drawn from Southeast Asia and Allied prisoners of war. The unsanitary conditions and mass movement of people during the construction of the Burma Railway, as depicted in Flanagan's novel, contributed significantly to the spread of infectious diseases such as cholera and typhoid in the region ("The Narrow Road to the Deep North' by Richard Flanagan"). The outbreak of cholera that originated in Burma has spread to various regions, including Manipur. This outbreak shows the devastating impact of the railway's construction on public health, as the unsanitary conditions created a fertile ground for disease transmission. Consequently, the spread of cholera from Burma to areas like Manipur suggests the far-reaching consequences of historical injustices.

Pabung Aribam's mother passed away in one of the villages on the outskirts of Imphal following a Japanese bombing while she was carrying her fourth child, so adding still another blow. After the death of Pabung's parents, a caring woman named Maharajkumari Phandengsana, who is lovingly called Kakaibemma, took care of him and his brothers. She had no biological children of her own, but she lovingly adopted Aribam's father.

Pabung writes about Kakaibemma in his book, *Living Shadows,* "The death of my father affected Maharajkumari Phandengsana (Kakaibemma), who adopted him and his three brothers, the most. Maharajkumari Phandengsana was the daughter of Chandrakriti Maharaj, the King of Manipur. She was a devout Vaishnavite who spent most of her time in meditation on Lord Gopaldeva. She and her husband, who was a titled royalty, did not have any issue of their own. Her husband died young and she was left alone with no immediate family…My father and three uncles addressed her as 'mother'" (Sharma, 2006.p.12).

In his book *Living Shadows*, Pabung Aribam recounts the deep bond he shared with Kakaibemma, who cared for him as if he were her own grandson. He describes how, as a child, he slept in her bed, only learning later that his mother, Borkanya, felt a quiet sorrow over not being able to nurse her firstborn herself. It was Kakaibemma who bathed and groomed him, and who took him along to various social and religious gatherings. Despite her age and his growing size, she continued to carry him on her back in the traditional Manipuri fashion, using a back strap made from a distinctive cloth called *nahong*. During their time in Radhakunda, Kakaibemma would descend from the balcony each evening to perform her prayers. The house's staircase, lacking any balustrades, posed a challenge for her failing eyesight, and it was during one of these descents, made without assistance, that she suffered an accident. It was her wish, like many Vaishnava, to die there" (Sharma, 2006.p.13).

As I was asking questions, Monjul Baruah, who accompanied me this time, nudged me, reminding me that it was time to change the battery. I looked over at Aribam, who was lost in thought, and gently asked him to take a moment to pause. It was then that he began to share his story. Just before his family was set to leave for Brindaban, he had lost his parents. In the midst of all that grief, he found a silver lining: the binding ties of family. His father had wisely connected two of his brothers with two of his mother's sisters, a move that brought everyone closer during this turbulent time. Among those uncles—

Gourachandra, Govardhan, and Krishnachandra—there was a profound sense of love and support that enveloped him and his siblings like a warm embrace. They taught him that being a parent extends far beyond blood; it's rooted in love, nurturing, and selfless acts. As the family honored his father's last wishes, moonlit nights turned into cherished memories, especially those with uncle Gourachandra, the talented singer and Jatra artist who kindled his passion for music. After nearly three years in Brindaban, his family made their way back to Manipur.

Aribam said, "As I reflect on the war's impact on my family, I realize it was a catalyst for change, forcibly uprooting us from our Manipur home and driving us into strange lands. We were faced with trials that tested our mettle, but ultimately, they tempered us, making us stronger. The war also ignited a fierce determination to survive in a world where scientific and technological advancements seemed to bypass us altogether. It was a jarring awakening to the complexity and vastness of the world, which I had previously underestimated. Before I could even venture out into the world, it came knocking on our doorstep, bringing with it a diverse array of nationalities - Japanese, Americans, British, Australians, and Africans. Their presence gave me a newfound perspective on my place in the grand pattern of things, and the stark reality that many of them had travelled far from their homes, only to find their eternal rest in our soil, left an indelible mark on my understanding of the world."

During the conversation, I realized that Pabung's account links personal loss with the broader cultural and social scenario of Manipur.

From Brindaban to Imphal

In the heart of Manipur, where the hills cradle whispers of ancient tales and the rivers hum melodies of a rich past, Aribam's formative years unfurl. Returning from the sacred land of Brindaban to Imphal, Aribam's journey enters an exciting chapter as he steps into the realm of education. Enrolling in a local primary school, and later he was admitted to the Johnstone High School. Johnston stood out as the crown jewel of high schools in his time. To gain admission to its esteemed institution, students were required to successfully complete a state-level entrance examination, a hurdle that Aribam overcame with distinction. Aribam fondly reminisces about a time when clocks and watches were mere fantasies in their home. Instead, they relied on the playful shadows of the morning sun to signal when it was time to prepare for school, and surprisingly, it worked quite well. Their daily adventure to school was a walk filled with laughter. Upon his arrival at Johnstone High School, he met the poet R.K. Surendrajit. Having spent some time in Santiniketan, he carried with him the profound influence of Rabindranath Tagore. Under his guidance, they learnt the melodies of Rabindra Sangeet as they prepared to share their voices in group songs. Surendrajit's teachings extended beyond mere academics; they were invitations to explore into the depths of one's soul, to discover unfamiliar zones of creativity.

"Music, I later realized, was my first and everlasting love," Pabung said. I watched *Baiju Bawra* (Crazy Baiju, 1952) more than a dozen times, not for the plot or the characters, but for the beautiful songs that lingered long after the credits rolled. Each time I stepped out of the cinema, the cool air embraced me like an old friend, and I would hum and sing, piecing together memories of the tunes.

This pattern persisted for some time, until Pabung's youngest uncle brought home a gramophone. By then, Aribam had begun to realize that relying solely on his earlier methods would not allow him to develop as a singer in the long term. After some reflection, he decided to seek formal singing lessons. Pabung remarked, "My exposure to Hindi film music had a profound, dual impact on me. First, listening to the legendary artists ignited a strong desire to seriously pursue Hindustani classical music. Second, I yearned to create music deeply rooted in my own culture rather than simply adopting influences from abroad. While these aspirations might seem contradictory, they actually complement each other. I quickly realized that without incorporating a personal, authentic touch into my technique and understanding, I would only become a mediocre Hindustani classical musician. I aspired to be both a singer and a composer."

He continued, "I began my journey in Hindustani classical music as part of my school curriculum under Oja Kunjo Singh, and after graduating, I continued my studies with Oja Mutum Modhu Singh. However, my passion for music wasn't fully supported at home. While my aunt and uncle appreciated music—my uncle being a singer himself—they worried that my interest might distract me from my academic pursuits. Their concerns were understandable, given that musicians and artists often face a challenging life. Success in this field is rare, and there's little room for mediocrity. I still remember the time I purchased a harmonium; my uncle quickly gave it away to someone else. Their intentions were rooted in concern, but it stifled my musical aspirations."

Forming an Artist: Aribam at Santiniketan

Pabung Aribam's eyes sparkled with excitement as he spoke about Santiniketan, a place that was nothing short of a beacon in his life's narrative. You could almost feel the energy shift as he reminisced about that formative period—a time when he made a bold stand against the conventional expectations of his traditional Indian family. Born into a world where a stable career in engineering was not just encouraged but almost required, he could have easily followed the well-trodden path toward security. Yet, as he carried the weight of those expectations, something inside him craved for a different kind of journey, one steeped in self-expression.

Aribam writes in the book *Living Shadow*, how he fell deeply in love with the beautiful environment of Santiniketan. He recalled that, without informing his family, he had embarked on a journey to West Bengal. He made a stop in Calcutta during the summer break, just before the academic session was to begin. From Calcutta, he took a train to Bolpur and then hired a rickshaw to complete his journey to Santiniketan. He remembered his first impression vividly, noting that as he approached the Ashram, he saw a road that was a lovely red color. Above the gate, it was written, "Ekameba Adityam", meaning "He is One, the Sun". These words deeply resonated with him, making him feel welcome and assuring him that he had arrived at the right place (Sharma, 2006)." Pabung Aribam then recalled a memorable moment that deepened his love for Santiniketan. From a distance, he saw a man working alone under the hot sun. Curious, he observed the man working diligently on a sculpture. The man would step back to view his work, but, seemingly dissatisfied, he would rush back and demolish it with a hammer. This cycle of creation and destruction was amazing to watch. Aribam later discovered that the man was the renowned artist Ramkinkar Beij.

"When I came to know him better, he never called me by my name. He called me "Naga boy" because he saw me dance in a Naga costume (Sharma, 2006)." By acknowledging Aribam's roots in Manipuri culture through his dance, Ramkinkar not only recognized the cultural heritage that Aribam carried but also affirmed the significance of local traditions in the broader artistic discourse. In Santiniketan, Pabung Aribam found himself immersed in an environment that celebrated creativity and intellectual exploration. The Ashram, founded by Rabindranath Tagore, served as a hub for artists, writers, and thinkers who sought to challenge conventions and push the boundaries of artistic expression. The aesthetic principles that Aribam absorbed during his time in Santiniketan would later manifest in his cinematic style. The influence of Santiniketan is evident in his ability to weave together local narratives with universal themes, allowing his films to resonate with a diverse audience.

His educational journey continued at Viswa-Bharati, Santiniketan, where he pursued both undergraduate and postgraduate studies. His deep interest in philosophy led him to the teachings of great minds, including the esteemed Prof. Kalidas Bhattacharya. In addition to philosophy, his time at Santiniketan allowed him to delve into the world of Rabindra Sangeet, classical music, and dance. "I studied Rabindra Sangeet for four years under the famous teachers Santi *da* and Konika *di*. The music Tagore, in its treatments of varied subjects and themes, made me realize the possibilities of the song form. This would become a lasting inspiration for my learning and understanding of the songs of Guru Dev (Sharma, 2006)."

Life in the ashram of Santiniketan was marked by simplicity, a simplicity that harmonized with the artistic and cultural ambiance of the place. The simplicity of life in Santiniketan offered him a new perspective. It taught him to appreciate the small joys and the beauty that exists in everyday moments. He learned that art is not merely an expression but a way of life—a means of connecting with the world and leaving an impact. The days spent in Santiniketan had the deepest influence on him as a person. It was here that he forged his identity, shaped by the experiences of loss, love, and art. The lessons he learned extended far beyond the classroom; they became the very fabric of his being. He came to understand that life is a journey filled with trials and tribulations, but it is also a canvas waiting to be painted with our experiences (Aribam Syam Sharma Collection | the Northeast India, n.d.).

Pabung Aribam said how he became interested in filmmaking. When he was studying at Viswa Bharati in Santiniketan from 1956 to 1960, he would go to Bolpur, a town nearby, to watch movies. Santiniketan didn't have movie theaters or a train station because Guru Dev (likely referring to Rabindranath Tagore) didn't want them there. One night, Pabung Aribam and his friends watched a movie called *Ajantrik* (The Unmechanical, 1958) by Ritwik Ghatak. After watching it, Pabung felt like he had a life-changing experience. It was like a revelation. The way the movie used images, time, and place deeply affected him. It made him feel that it was the kind of film he wanted to create himself.

Pabung said that Santiniketan shaped his artistic outlook. It had given him the insight into the different possibilities of looking at the world. It gave him the courage and temperament that artistic pursuits relentlessly demand. If not for his good fortune to be in Santiniketan, he dared say that his life would have been different. He owed to Santiniketan the seeds of all his creative works. The simple life of the Ashram had honed in him the ability to take life as a celebration and the courage to challenge the difficulties it threw up. It was here, apart from the academics of philosophy, that he developed a personal philosophy that gave him the ability to appreciate life in its splendored diversity (Sharma, 2006).

The journey of Aribam Syam Sharma to Santiniketan is a fascinating story of artistic learning, cultural identification, and the search for passion. It expresses the challenges and victories faced by an artist who is dealing with family and society's expectations while staying true to his inner calling. His experiences in Santiniketan not only helped to define his identity as a filmmaker but also prepared him for his contributions to Manipuri film and the larger debate on cultural representation in Indian films.

From lectures to life lessons

Pabung Aribam leaned back in his chair, the creak of the wood punctuating the silence as he paused for a moment, reflecting on those days. You could see the nostalgia wash over him, mixed with a flicker of uncertainty. "You know," he began again, "when I came back to Manipur after my days at Santiniketan, it felt like stepping into a tug-of-war. On one side, my dreams were pulling me, and on the other, my family was doing everything they could to keep me in a comforting embrace." He chuckled softly, shaking his head at the memory of his aunt, *Inamma*, and uncle. "They had this whole dramatic pitch of emotional blackmail lined up. I mean, who knew a fit of 'illness' could turn into such a masterful ruse? They were sure that if I went back, I'd get swept up in my ambitions and forget all about them."

The warmth in his eyes turned a shade serious as he continued. "But here's the kicker: I realized that I owed them. They had taken care of me, loved me, and sacrificed so much. So, when the opportunity arose to teach Maths at Tombisana High School, I jumped at it. After all, it seemed practical, you know." But then, tragedy struck. Quote: "Only three months after starting the job, something unexpected happened. Prof. Dhananjoy, who taught philosophy at DM College, suddenly died. I remember that day clearly. It was a shock. He lived right next door, so it was completely unexpected."

He wiped a hand across his face, as if shaking off the weight of those memories. "That loss opened a door, though. The principal needed someone to step in, and, my name came up. Prof. S. Chakravarti, who had a pretty stellar reputation, called me, and Prof. E. Nilakanta Singh, a formidable figure in literature, put in a good word. Next thing I knew, I was sitting in the principal's office, and there wasn't even a formal interview!"

Pabung laughed, a light sound that broke the seriousness of his recollections. "It's hard to believe, but after teaching math for a short time, I unexpectedly became a philosophy lecturer. It felt strange, like a sudden change in direction, but somehow it felt right."

He leaned forward now, excitement creeping back into his voice. "Then I had to take the UPSC exam, which was tough. I needed to pass it to keep my job as a lecturer. When I finally did, it was a huge relief. I was officially a lecturer with a real salary!" He paused, remembering the busy college days. "That job security was incredibly important. It allowed me to support my family and also gave me the chance to enjoy my passions: music and theater."

Pabung Aribam settled back again, a glimmer of satisfaction in his eyes. "Life has a way of surprising us, doesn't it? I would have never imagined I'd be teaching philosophy after math, but here I am."

Here, I must mention the new life as husband and father. Pabung Aribam married Gurumayum

Radhapyari Devi in 1963, and they built a loving family together. They have four children: two sons, Aribam Gautam Sharma and Aribam Uttam Sharma, and two daughters, Aribam Gayatri Devi and Aribam Geetanjali Devi. Each of their children has their own unique qualities and contributions to the family. Pabung lives in the neighbourhood of Thangmeiband Lourung Purel Leikai, in the heart of Imphal, Manipur. This is more than just a place of residence for him; it's a thriving community filled with a treasure full of memories and connections that have been passed down through generations, deeply rooted in the family's rich heritage and values.

M.K. Binodini: collaboration leads to innovation

I've always been captivated by the life and work of Maharaj Kumari Binodini Devi. It's amazing how someone from such a royal background could impact the world of literature and cinema so profoundly. I remember this one time, I was conversing with Pabung Aribam, and he said something that really stuck with me, "Her collaboration with me was crucial for the growth of Manipuri cinema." Those words just opened my eyes to how instrumental she was in shaping that landscape.

Can you imagine growing up as a princess in Manipur? Despite her royal status, she had this incredible ability to blend tradition with modern ideas in her writing. Her literary contributions were not just significant; they were transformative. She wrote novels, short stories, and even award-winning screenplays. She was awarded the Padma Shri award in 1976. And then there is her historical novel *Boro Saheb Ongbi Sanatombi*. For which she won the Sahitya Akademi Award in 1979. It was later translated into English as *The Princess and the Political Agent* in 2020.

L Somi Roy writes about MK Binodini in his article, "Binodini's Women: The three strong characters of *My Son, My Precious*" as published inn The Indian Express on March 9, 2018, "MK Binodini, who published under the single name of Binodini is noted for the centrality of women in all her work. It is not at the expense of men. There are no bad men in her writing, just complex characters, sometimes clueless dolts, but never villains. It may be said that Binodini admits to only one true villain in all her creations – her doll Ati. As the youngest daughter of Maharaja Sir Churachand Singh (1891-1941) and Maharani Dhanamanjuri Devi, Binodini often said that the palace staff used to eavesdrop when she played with her dolls. Her dolls' colourful characters and the accompanying running dialogue gave them distinctive lives and destinies. They became a precursor to the snappy exchanges and characterisations, the hallmark of Binodini's film and literary creations."

I remember sitting with Pabung, overflowing with curiosity about this remarkable lady. I asked him heaps of questions, and he shared some fascinating insights, "Maharaj Kumari Binodini, or M.K.

Binodini, as we often call her, was the youngest of five daughters of Maharaj Churachand and Maharani Dhanamanjuri. You know, I used to call her as Sana Ebemma out of affection. She was one of the greatest writers from Manipur." Pabung continued, "then came the day I met her for the first time, it was pure magic. It was during the year we celebrated Guru Dev's birth centenary, and excitement filled the air. I had just put my heart and soul into a stage adaptation of Guru Dev's work, *Raktakarabi* (The Red Oleanders), directed by Ojah Nilamani. I played the character "Bishu Pagla," and I was so nervous yet exhilarated! After the curtains fell, I was backstage, when suddenly, there she was, rushing towards me. "You brought Bishu to life!" she exclaimed. I could hardly believe she saw my performance that way. That single moment turned into the beginning of something truly special between us.

Pabung continued, "Even though I was already well entrenched in the world of Manipuri cinema, Binodini had yet to begin. I had directed my first film and was working on the second, but I knew we had to collaborate. So, I approached her to write a song.' At first, she seemed hesitant, but I could see a flicker of interest in her eyes. Eventually, she agreed to write a song for the film *Matamgi Manipur*. And I still remember her saying, 'Once I started, I found joy in it!' That was music to my ears!"

Pabung Aribam told me that after that, he asked her to write the script for his film, *Olangthagee*

Wangmadasoo. She accepted, and honestly, it opened a whole new world for both of them. She later adapted a short radio play into the script for another film, *Imagi Ningthem*. "The energy between us was exciting, and we both learned so much from each other," said Pabung. Pabung made a documentary on the life and creative journey of M.K. Binodini, where Binodini states, "Filming of Manipuri films started in 1971. I associated in writing lyrics, taking care of costumes. Later I teamed up with Syam Sharma. We made films like *Imagi Ningthem*, *Ishanou*, *Paokhum Ama*, *Olangthagee Wangmadasoo*. Something that I was happy about is that I did not consider writing film script as separate work… I worked in documentary films too. I wrote scripts for Orchids of Manipur. I loved Orchids of Manipur. Typical of Manipur."

M.K. Binodini comments on working with Pabung Aribam in the documentary on Aribam Syam Sharma, directed by G. Nirmal Sharma. She states, "When I write scripts for his films, there are days and days of discussion with him. We throw suggestions and ideas at each other. The discussions are intense, and in the end, I cannot figure out who made which suggestion. At these moments, we achieve a level of communication that is extraordinary."

Similarly, Pabung Aribam says about Binodini in the book, *Living Shadows*, "In our long and fruitful collaboration, we act as a catalyst for each other for the generation of ideas and discovery through discussions. During these discussions and general conversations if any idea emerges we latch on to it and explore deeper into it. And as she often says, at the end, we can not delineate which idea was whose because we had reached an uncommon and extraordinary level of communication. Dialogues between us have been the beginning of much of the screenplays. My best films owe much to her commitments. It is not to easy to describe the dynamics that works well but it must lie in our trust for one another and sincerity of our friendship" (p.32).

The following films prove to the remarkable creative partnership between Pabung and M. K. Binodini. Their collaboration made history and enhanced the landscape of Manipuri cinema. Notable among these works are *Olangthagee Wangmadasoo*, directed by Aribam Syam Sharma with the screenplay and story written by M. K. Binodini Devi; *Imagi Ningthem*, directed by Aribam Syam Sharma and again featuring a screenplay and story by M. K. Binodini Devi; and *Paukam Ama*, *Ishanou*, *Sanabi*, *Ashangba Nongjabi*, and *Nongphadok Lakpa Atithi*, all directed by Aribam Syam Sharma and written by M. K. Binodini Devi. Even in the documentary *Orchids of Manipur*, the co-ordination of Aribam Syam Sharma's direction and Binodini Devi's writing shines through. These films show their significant contributions and represent the profound artistic collaboration that had between the them.

Understanding that "collaboration leads to innovation" changed their method of generating ideas and approaching problem solutions. Every meeting turned into a chance to explore fresh concepts and challenge accepted norms. Combining their various experiences and skills helped them reach a shared vision for their work and solve problems. It results in works that have had a lasting influence on both audiences and the history of cinema in the region.

***

Works Cited

Aribam Syam Sharma Collection | The Northeast India. (n.d.). The Northeast India. https://www.nearchive.in/aribam-syam-sharma-collection

Sharma Aribam Syam, *Living Shadows*, (published by Gauhati Cine Club, Assam, First Edition, 2006) 12. 13. 19. 22.23. 24. 32.

Tony's Book World, 30 Aug. 2014. https://anokatony.blog/2014/08/31/the-narrow-road-to-the-deep-north-by-richard-flanagan/

Chapter Three

1970s: Aribam's Iconic 3

During the 1970s, Manipur, a state with enormous cultural diversity, was witnessing a fascinating cinematic scene grow. The local people was captivated by commercial films, especially Hindi films coming from the booming Bollywood industry. Movie theaters in Imphal, the heart of Manipur, were crowded with enthusiastic audience eager to immerse themselves in the larger-than-life dramas. Although it offered entertainment, this predominance of Hindi films also presented a threat to the fledgling Manipuri cinema, which struggled to attract the interest of its own people. Against this background, a visionary filmmaker Aribam Syam Sharma became an influential figure set to change the course of Manipuri cinema. Understanding the general tastes of the local audiences, Pabung Aribam set out to make films that would appeal to them. His method was precisely combining, into his own films, elements that defined commercial cinema, including more melodrama, captivating song and dance sequences, and interesting narratives. This approach aimed to bridge the gap between the familiar entertainment offered by Bollywood and the untapped potential of Manipuri filmmaking.

Pabung's vision materialized in the form of three landmark feature films that would not only fascinate audiences but also redefine the landscape of Manipuri cinema: *Lamja Parshuram* (1974), *Saphabee* (1976), and *Olangthagee Wangmadasoo* (Even Beyond the Summer Horizon, 1979). These films were meticulously made to appeal to the local audience's tastes while gently exposing them to Manipur's distinctive unique traditions and stories. The impact of Pabung Aribam's three films was profound and far-reaching. They achieved unprecedented box office success, breaking records for the longest theatrical runs of Manipuri films. More importantly, they instilled a sense of pride and confidence in the local audience, demonstrating that Manipuri filmmakers were capable of making films that were just as entertaining and engaging as those from Bollywood. Pabung instilled a belief that Manipuri filmmakers could match the standards of Bollywood, thus boosting local pride and interest in their own cinema. This realization sparked a renewed interest in Manipuri cinema, paving the way for a new generation of filmmakers to explore their own stories and share them with the world.

Lamja Parshuram: Manipur's Blockbuster

Aribam Syam Sharma made his debut feature film, *Lamja Parshuram* (1974), which was produced by G. Narayan Sharma. The film is based on the play *Lamja Parshuram*, written by the renowned Manipuri dramatist G.C. Tongbra. This film was a significant departure from traditional Manipuri cinema, incorporating elements of popular storytelling, such as songs and action sequences. However, Aribam made sure to stay true to his roots by infusing the story with Manipuri culture and traditions. The film's success ran for 100 days in theaters, making it a significant feat in Manipuri cinema. Film critic Meghachandra Kongbam writes in his book, *Manipuri Cinema*, "During the period, Raj Kapoor's super hit film, *Bobby* was screened at Usha Cinema in Imphal, but could not get the momentum of *Lamja Parshuram. Thus, Lamja Parshuram* snatched away the Manipuri audience away from Bollywood cinema. It ran for 15 weeks with the celebration of 100 days" (p.73).

In the narrative of *Lamja Parshuram*, the protagonist Parshuram is depicted as a spirited young man in his mid-twenties, whose life is profoundly affected by the absence of his parents and the turmoil caused by his uncle-in-law, Thambaljao. The backstory reveals that Parshuram's father, Vikram, departed for London to pursue a degree in law, leaving behind a pregnant wife, Leibaklei. During this time, Leibaklei depended on the financial support Vikram sent. However, Maama Thambaljao, her uncle-in-law, misused these funds, resulting in dire consequences for Leibaklei and her unborn child. The situation escalates when Maama Thambaljao forcibly sells Leibaklei to an unknown contractor. In a desperate struggle against her captor, Leibaklei kills Thambaljao in self-defense when he attempts to assault her. Fleeing the scene to evade suspicion, she escapes to

Nabadweep, thereby leaving her child, Parshuram, in an orphaned state.

Thus begins Parshuram's quest for identity and belonging. After running away, he faces a traumatic accident with a truck, which leads to his adoption by the truck driver. This encounter marks a pivotal moment in his life, where he is given a semblance of family while simultaneously severing his ties to his birth family. As he grows up, he becomes a driver, forming a close bond with his friend Tomal, who represents loyalty and camaraderie amidst Parshuram's chaotic life. In a turn of fate, Parshuram learns that Maama Thambaljao resides in Moreh. Fueled by rage and a desire for retribution, he travels to confront Thambaljao, leading to an immediate and aggressive encounter. This moment encapsulates Parshuram's internal struggle: the conflicting emotions of vengeance intertwined with his yearning for familial connection. Also, Parshuram's romantic interest, Indrani, plays a significant role in the unfolding events. Her father, who befriends Parshuram's long-lost father, serves as a catalyst for familial reunification. This man treats both Parshuram and Indrani as his own children, providing a nurturing environment that contrasts sharply with Parshuram's tumultuous upbringing.

Despite this newfound familial connection, Parshuram grapples with a childhood vow he made: to kill his father upon discovering his whereabouts. Parshuram's refusal to acknowledge this father figure intensifies the tension between his desire for vengeance and the possibility of reconciliation. Ultimately, the narrative culminates in the return of Leibaklei from Nabadweep to console Parshuram, indicating a potential resolution to his internal conflict.

Saphabee: Loktak's Echo

Pabung Aribam's second feature film, *Saphabee* (1976), the first Manipuri folk film, was a game-changer in more ways than one. Produced by G. Narayan Sharma, it was the first Manipuri folk film. Based on the traditional Manipuri play, *Haorang Leishang Saaphabee*, the film showcased the state's rich cultural heritage to the world. To make the film feel more local, Pabung composed the songs in the tune of Manipuri folk songs, adding an authentic touch to the narrative. Kongbam (2021) writes that Aribam Syam Sharma's second feature film, *Saphabee (*1976) is a period movie from a different era. It reflects the past civilization of Manipuri society. It explores the rich, typical culture and tradition, and ancient literature of the past. It depicts that the great treasure of Manipuri culture came into existence since the time of immemorial when the Gods and the human used to live together (p.73).

The film *Saphabee* is a timeless tale of love, sacrifice, and tragedy set against the beautiful backdrop of the Loktak Lake, where two regions, Khuman and Kege, hold not only the physical space but also the essence of deep cultural ties. At the heart of this poignant narrative lies the immortal love story of Loya Naha Saphaba, the cherished son of King Thongnang of the Khuman region, and Haorang Leishang Saphabee, the beloved daughter of Tabung, the noble king of Kege.

The film intricately weaves the destinies of these two royal families, whose friendship flourishes across the shimmering waters of Loktak Lake. A bond of camaraderie exists between the two kings, echoing promises of unity and a future intertwining of their bloodlines through a matrimonial alliance envisioned for their yet-to-be-born children. This dream, however, is tragically shattered by a series of misunderstandings and fateful events. In a harrowing twist, Tabung, blinded by the fear of invasion, mistakenly perceives Saphaba as an enemy intruder and, in a moment of misguided aggression, takes his life. The depth of despair deepens when Saphabee, unable to bear the weight of her loss, chooses to follow her beloved into the afterlife, taking her own life in an act of heartbreaking devotion.

The film culminates in a dramatic confrontation as the grieving Kings, Thongnang and Tabung, in their anguish, decide to end their own lives in a duel—a tragic pursuit of retribution and solidarity in grief. As the winds of fate swirl around them, the skies darken, and the thunderous voice of Khamnung Kikoi Louonbee, the goddess of death, reverberates through the heavens. With a powerful intervention, she halts their duel, shaking the very foundations of their sorrow with a command that echoes through the stormy skies. In a divine revelation, Saphaba and Saphabee are then shown ascending to the heavens, transcending their mortal pain and sorrow, finally united at the feet of their God, symbolizing eternal love that defies the boundaries of life and death.

Released on July 13, 1976, at Usha Cinema, *Saphabee* remains etched in the hearts of audiences, capturing the profound themes of love, tragedy, and the mystical connection between the two realms. The film went on to win the award for Best Feature Film in Manipuri at the 24th National Film Awards.

Olangthagee Wangmadasoo: The Film That Conquered *Sholay*

One of his most notable films, the third feature film of Aribam, *Olangthagee Wangmadasoo* (Even Beyond the Summer Horizon, 1979), became a super hit in Manipuri cinema. Released at Friends Talkies in Imphal on January 8, 1980 that ran for 32 weeks in Imphal, it broke the previous record held by the Hindi film *Sholay* (1975) which lasted for 28 weeks. It became the longest running film till date in the history of Manipuri Cinema. The film's enduring success can be attributed to its universal theme – a timeless love story that transcends the boundaries of language and culture. The film won the award for Best Regional Film at the 27th National Film Festival in 1980.

Kongbam (2021) writes that *Olangthagee Wangmadasoo* became the all-time blockbuster and the longest running Manipuri film in the history of Manipuri cinema. Kongbam further added that it was made on the first original screenplay of renowned Manipuri writer M.K. Binodini, Padmashree and Sahitya Akademi awardee. It was well- crafted film with box office elements infused with regional flavor. It contained eight songs (p.75).

The film intricately weaves the romantic narrative of Bijay and Thadoi, who are deeply in love and intent on marrying each other. Their initial encounter unfolds at a musical night. Bijay, a gifted singer, captivates Thadoi, a medical student who has a passion for poetry. Thadoi's poems resonate with Bijay, who melodically adapts them. Bijay finds himself torn between the aspirations of his grandparents. His grandfather, embodying traditional values, advocates for Bijay to learn swordsmanship, a skill reflective of valour and strength. In contrast, his grandmother encourages him to pursue music, signifying a duality in cultural education that mirrors the broader societal divide regarding gender roles and personal aspirations. Both grandparents are adamant about marital prospects for Bijay, emphasising the pressures exerted by lineage and societal expectations. Conversely, Thadoi's familial context adds another layer of conflict to their love story. Her brother, Kamaljit, along with his wife, exemplifies the societal ambition for upward mobility by advocating for Thadoi to marry Jiten, a wealthy family friend. This contrast shows the societal tension between love and economic advantage, as Kamaljit's intentions appear to prioritise material well-being over Thadoi's personal happiness.

The film's narrative arc intensifies when Thadoi elopes with Bijay, an act of defiance against her family's ambitions. However, their union is thwarted when Kamaljit deceitfully agrees to perform the kanyadaan—a sacred ritual signifying the giving away of the bride—only to subsequently betray his promise. The assassination of Bijay's grandfather by Kamaljit's goon introduces a critical turning point in the narrative— themes of honour, loss, and the violent intersections of family loyalty and betrayal. Despite the myriad challenges they face, including Bijay's life-threatening attack, his grandfather's death, and the motif of pilgrimage—often symbolizing both physical and spiritual journeys—the resilience of Bijay and Thadoi's love remains unyielding. At the end, the film goes through a landscape fraught with misunderstandings and conflicts, ultimately culminating in a reconciliatory resolution where Bijay and Thadoi rediscover their love. This reconnection not only signifies the triumph of personal affection over societal constraints but also underscores the importance of communication and understanding in overcoming adversities.

Olangthagee Wangmadasoo's success among the Manipuri audience served as a pivotal moment for Aribam, prompting a profound shift in his cinematic aspirations. Initially, the driving force behind his filmmaking was a deep-seated concern for the very survival of Manipuri cinema in the 1970s. Pabung Aribam, a philosophy lecturer at the time, faced a discouraging reality: a limited number of cinema houses, low audience turnout for Manipuri language films, the considerable expense of traveling to Calcutta for studio facilities, and the absence of a viable market. These challenges painted a grim picture, making the prospect of making Manipuri films seem almost impossible.

However, a critical change in perspective occurred when, after *Olangthagee Wangmadasoo*'s success, Pabung came to believe in the potential for Manipuri cinema to not only survive but also thrive. This realization liberated him to pursue a more meaningful form of filmmaking, one deeply connected to Manipuri culture and tradition. Pabung's films then became driven by a desire to express his cultural heritage through cinema, rather than just keeping the industry afloat. This marked a transition from survival-oriented filmmaking to the creation of films with artistic and cultural significance.

Work Cited

Kongbam, M. (2021). *Manipuri cinema* (1st ed.). Ningthoukhongjam Ranjanas Devi & Wangkhei Ningthem Pukhri Mapal, Imphal.

Chapter Four

Two Films, One Legacy

During the 1970s and 80s, a wave of filmmakers in India spearheaded a "new cinema" movement, challenging the established norms of mainstream storytelling. Directors like Shyam Benegal, Adoor Gopalakrishan, Jahnu Barua, M.S. Sathyu, Govind Nihalani, Mani Kaul, Kumar Shahani, Saeed Mirza and others pushed boundaries, experimenting with innovative forms and tackling previously unexplored subjects. This departure was a conscious effort to move away from conventional narratives, focusing on social realism and deeper thematic exploration. Mani Kaul's *Uski Roti* (Other's bread,1969) symbolized this shift, offering a minimalist cinematic experience with minimal dialogue. Similarly, Kumar Shahani's *Maya Darpan* (The Illusory Mirror,1972), examined the societal changes accompanying India's transition from feudalism. M.S. Sathyu's *Garam Hawa* (Scorching Winds, 1973) faced the sensitive issue of the partition, portraying the struggles of Muslim families dealing with the difficult decision of whether to migrate to Pakistan or remain in India.

In late 1960s/early 1970s India, post-Partition issues, regionalism, and socio-economic disparities fuelled social and political unrest. This context gave rise to the Indian New Wave, a cinematic movement that rejected Bollywood's escapism and formulas, embracing realism and authentic depictions of daily life. This new wave of cinema aimed to reflect the complexities of Indian society, offering nuanced perspectives and artistic innovations seeking alternative cinematic experiences.

Mani Kaul's film *Uski Roti* (1969) characterises the experimental ethos of New Cinema. With minimal dialogue and a contemplative pace, *Uski Roti* challenges conventional narrative structures. The film's focus on the mundane aspects of life—a woman's daily chores and the rhythm of her existence—creates a meditative experience for the viewer. Kaul's approach invites audiences to engage with the film on a sensory level, emphasizing the importance of visual storytelling over verbal exposition. This radical departure from dialogue-driven narratives laid the groundwork for future filmmakers to explore new cinematic languages. Kumar Shahani's *Maya Darpan* (1972) further shows this trend of experimentation. The film addresses the transition from feudal social structures to a more liberal state, reflecting the socio-political changes occurring in India during that period. Through its fragmented narrative and rich visual symbolism, *Maya Darpan* critiques the socio-cultural landscape of its time, challenging viewers to reconsider their understanding of identity and reality. M.S. Sathyu's *Garam Hawa* (1973) is another seminal work within the

New Cinema movement, addressing the complexities of identity and belonging in the context of the Partition. The film explores the struggles faced by Muslim families who were torn between the decision to migrate to Pakistan or remain in India. Sathyu's sensitive handling of this poignant issue, combined with a focus on the human cost of political decisions, elevates *Garam Hawa* beyond mere historical narrative to a deeply emotional exploration of loss and resilience. The film's realistic portrayal of characters and their dilemmas resonates with the audience, creating a powerful commentary on the socio-political landscape of post-Partition India. Sathyu's ability to weave personal stories within the broader historical context exemplifies the New Cinema's commitment to social relevance and emotional depth.

Shyam Benegal's *Ankur* (The Seedling/1974) is a landmark film that delves into the entrenched caste and feudal systems in rural India. The story revolves around a young couple who become embroiled in a power struggle with a tyrannical landlord. Through its nuanced characterization and compelling narrative, *Ankur* highlights the struggles of the oppressed and underscores the necessity for social change. The film's ending, which suggests that the exploited have the agency to rise against their oppressors, serves as a powerful message of hope and resistance. Benegal's focus on caste politics and rural dynamics reflects the New Cinema's commitment to addressing pressing social issues, offering a voice to marginalized communities often overlooked in mainstream narratives.

Adoor Gopalakrishnan's *Swayamvaram* (1972) marks a significant departure from traditional Indian filmmaking conventions. By eschewing songs, dances, and melodrama, Gopalakrishnan crafts a narrative centred on the internal struggles of his protagonist. The film explores themes of choice and autonomy, particularly in the context of marriage and societal expectations. Through its minimalist approach and rich visual language, *Swayamvaram* invites viewers to reflect on the complexities of personal agency within a conservative societal framework. Gopalakrishnan's emphasis on character development and psychological depth exemplifies the New Cinema's focus on realism and introspection, setting a benchmark for future filmmakers.

Girish Kasaravalli's *Ghatashraaddha* (The Ritual, 1977), a Kannada-language film, is a stark portrayal of societal hypocrisy and female suppression within a rigid Brahminical structure. The film centers on Udupa, a traditional scholar and his widowed daughter, Yamuna. Yamuna's secret relationship with a school teacher and her resulting pregnancy reveal the deep contradictions present in the community's moral standards. While Udupa is away, the villagers' actions highlight their firm adherence to tradition and their harsh condemnation of Yamuna. The narrative examines the consequences of societal pressures, as Yamuna's exclusion, the abortion arranged by her lover, and Udupa's symbolic performance of her last rites indicate the limited agency offered to women. School teacher's brief support contrasts with the societal cruelty Yamuna faces, ultimately leading to her abandonment. The ending of the film, captured in Yamuna's shaved head and solitude, serves as a powerful commentary on the human cost of blind adherence to tradition.

In the 1980s, Jahnu Barua emerged as a significant voice in Assamese cinema, contributing to the New Cinema movement with films that conveyed a distinctively Assamese identity. His debut film, *Aparoopa* (1982), stands out for its exploration of a young married woman's quest for independence in a patriarchal society. Barua's narrative challenges traditional gender roles and highlights the struggles faced by women in conservative cultures. By focusing on her journey against the backdrop of societal constraints, Barua's work resonates with broader themes of identity and self-discovery. His ability to convey the complexities of Assamese culture while addressing universal human experiences underscores the New Cinema's commitment to regional narratives that transcend geographical boundaries.

Redefining Manipuri Cinema

In the context of Manipur's cinematic landscape, the 1980s marked a pivotal turning point with the emergence of Aribam Syam Sharma. Through a deliberate departure from the conventional popular genres, Aribam spearheaded a cinematic renaissance in Manipuri cinema, laying the groundwork for the New Cinema movement in the state. This paradigmatic shift was not only a response to the stagnation of the cinema in the region but also a proof to Pabung Aribam's commitment to exploring themes and narrative techniques that could elevate the art form. His choice to veer away from commercially viable projects and pursue meaningful, realistic cinema was met with skepticism and ridicule by some contemporaries. Nevertheless, he challenged the status quo by making films that expressed his unique vision. As he recalled, this courageous approach was driven by a deep concern for the survival and identity of Manipuri cinema as a distinctive artistic expression.

Through his epoch-making films, Pabung not only redefined the limits of Manipuri cinema but also catapulted it onto the global cinematic map, leaving an indelible mark on the industry. His works bridged cultural narratives with universal themes, showcasing the rich cultural scenario of Manipur while addressing broader human experiences. With each film, he demonstrated an unwavering dedication to authentic storytelling, effectively narrating the complexities of life in Manipur.

Pabung has secured his place as a vanguard of Manipuri cinema, inspiring generations of filmmakers to follow in his footsteps. Through his pioneering efforts, he not only elevated the industry but also instigated a movement aimed at revitalizing meaningful storytelling, establishing Manipuri cinema as a distinctive art form with a notable global presence. His legacy continues to influence contemporary filmmakers, reminding them of the power of cinema as a medium for cultural expression and social commentary.

The filmmakers associated with the New Cinema movement have left an indelible mark on the landscape of Indian cinema. Their contributions not only redefined cinematic language but also paved the way for future generations of filmmakers to explore complex themes and narratives. The movement's emphasis on realism, social relevance, and character-driven storytelling continues to influence contemporary Indian cinema, inspiring filmmakers to engage with pressing social issues and challenge societal norms. Moreover, the New Cinema movement facilitated a greater appreciation for regional and independent filmmaking, allowing diverse voices and narratives to emerge. This shift has led to a richer cinematic landscape, where the complexities of Indian society can be explored from multiple perspectives.

Pabung Aribam's Two Masterpieces

Aribam Syam Sharma's contributions to Manipuri cinema represent a pivotal moment in the evolution of regional Indian cinema, marking an era that not only highlights the unique cultural narratives of Manipur but also places them on an international platform. His two landmark films, *Imagi Ningthem* (My Son, My Precious, 1981), and *Ishanou* (The Chosen One, 1990), have significantly influenced both the aesthetic and thematic development of Manipuri filmmaking, that established its significance in the global cinematic landscape. *Imagi Ningthem*, considered the cornerstone of modern Manipuri cinema, was a groundbreaking achievement recognized far beyond the regional context. It garnered the prestigious Grand Prix at the Festival of Three Continents in Nantes, France, in 1982, making it the first Manipuri and North-East film to receive accolades at an international film festival. This appreciation not only gave the Manipuri film more credibility in a larger sense but also pointed out the creative possibilities of regional stories in the international film scene. The film's subsequent accolades, including the Rajat Kamal and the Best Child Artist award for Master Leikhendra at the 29th National Film Awards, proved its legacy and demonstrated the prowess of local talent on national and international stages.

The 1990s marked a significant turning point for Manipuri cinema, especially with the release of *Ishanou* (The Chosen One). This film was prominently featured in the Un Certain Regard section at the 44th Cannes Film Festival in 1991. The narrative of *Ishanou* centers around the Maibi tradition, exploring the complexities of gender, spirituality, and societal roles within Manipuri lore. By choosing such a culturally rich and layered theme, Pabung not only introduced a broader audience to the Maibi phenomenon but also challenged the predominantly patriarchal narratives in Indian cinema. The film's distinct portrayal of female agency and spiritual embodiment was met with critical acclaim, culminating in the film receiving the Rajat Kamal for Best Regional Film (Best Feature Film in Each of the Language Other Than Those Specified in the Schedule VIII of the Constitution), alongside a Special Mention for lead actress Anoubam Kiranmala at the 38th National Film Awards.

Imagi Ningthem: Reflection of technical critique and cultural appreciation

The film *Imagi Ningthem* (1981), filmed with a handheld 16mm Bolex camera and subsequently enlarged to 35mm, is a poignant portrayal of the complexities of human relationships, set against the rural backdrop of Manipur. The film begins with a sequence of a woman, Dhani, traveling in a rickshaw. She is going to work as a school teacher in a remote area of Manipur. The following words, used as the exposition of the story, are heard in the background: "I am going to work in a village far away, as a teacher in a small school. I need to work. I need a job. How will I manage otherwise? My family situation compels it. I got this permanent job with great difficulty. Those in need cannot be choosy." She reaches the village and stays at Gandhar's house, an assistant teacher at the school. In the school, she quickly notices Thoithoi, a bright but troubled student, whose grandfather, Pupu, asks Dhani to tutor him. Dhani agrees, drawn to the boy's curiosity but sensing a hidden sorrow. Gandhar reveals Thoithoi's tragic family history: his mother, Memtombi, was seduced and abandoned by an officer, dying during childbirth. Dhani, now aware of Thoithoi's emotional burden, dedicates herself to helping him heal. Shaken, Dhani discovers the officer, Dinachandra, is her cousin's husband. Though Dinachandra is away, Dhani shares the tragic story with Ekashini (Dinachandra's wife), who initially struggles to accept the truth. Driven by empathy, Ekashini attempts to meet Thoithoi, but misses him the first time. On her second visit, Thoithoi mistakes her for his mother, begging her to stay and shedding tears. Though she leaves, Ekashini is deeply affected by his pain.

The following day, Thoithoi waits by the road, his heart hoping. But his wait is in vain, and his health takes a turn for the worse. Here, I would like to mention that I feel a profound connection between the filmmaker's early loss of his biological parents and Thoithoi's yearning for his mother. Through Thoithoi's longing, it seems that Pabung Aribam channels his own deep emotions. As he shared with me in a personal communication (30 April, 2025): "Yes, the pain, emotions, and feelings regarding the loss of my parents in childhood are always with me, and perhaps Thoithoi's longing for his mother mirrors my loss. My heart still longs for the day I can see my mother again."

In the film, we can see Ekashini, her maternal instincts fully awakened, rushes to Thoithoi's side as he is ill. She brings him to her home, seeking medical help. Pupu, fearing the boy's displacement, wants to keep him away. Dhani urges Ekashini to return Thoithoi, but instead, she proposes enrolling him in a local school. Ekashini pours her love into caring for Thoithoi, and the bond between them blossoms, stronger with each passing day. Meanwhile, Dinachandra returns home and, sensing a shift in his wife, inquires about Thoithoi. Ekashini, shielding him from the full truth, explains that she has adopted the boy out of love, assuring him that there will be no future issues. When she reveals that the boy is from Dhani's village, Dinachandra insists on contacting Dhani to arrange for the child's return.

In this narrative, Ekashini takes Thoithoi to the Raas Leela dance at a Hindu temple, where he would play the role of Lord Krishna. The plot sets when Pupu arrives, intent on reclaiming Thoithoi, and confronts Dinachandra, expressing his emotional turmoil over the prospect of his grandson being raised by someone who has shown indifference to their own offspring. Holding Thoithoi in his lap, he says to Ekashini, "I have something to say to you. You may not know that my daughter has wronged you. But you sheltered my grandson. Nothing pleases me more. But I feel, it is not proper for my grandson to stay here. Don't be angry. I wish to take my grandson with me today. The Sahib knows…"

Pupu's insistence on bringing Thoithoi home ends in Ekashini's confrontation with her husband Dinachandra and she passionately resists his decision. In a moment of frustration, she expresses her indignation, questioning how two individuals- Pupu and Dinachandra- could make such a significant choice without seeking her permission. Following this outburst, she rushes out of the house, seizes Thoithoi by the hand, and departs.

The filmmaker Aribam composes a poignant frame: in the foreground, we see Dinachandra leaning against the door; in the middle of the frame sits Pupu on the porch; and in the background, Ekashini is depicted as she holds Thoithoi's shoulders while they leave. This composition carries profound symbolic significance particularly through the positioning of the three central characters: Dinachandra, Pupu, and Ekashini. Each figure serves as a complex representation of themes such as responsibility, abandonment, and the quest for redemption, building a layered narrative within a single frame. Dinachandra, positioned in the foreground, symbolizes abandonment and guilt. Leaning against the door, he represents a figure who has rejected his responsibilities; he betrayed Pupu's daughter, who died during childbirth and it shows his role as a coward. His physical posture, leaning and almost out of the frame, reflects his moral withdrawal from the consequences of his actions and suggests the emotional void left in the live of the woman affected by his decisions. Pupu, seated in the middle of the frame, represents strength and the burden of maternal care. As the sole guardian of her deceased daughter's son, he symbolises loyalty. His position in the centre signifies his role as a stabilizing force amid the chaos wrought by Dinachandra's abandonment. Pupu's experience illustrates the complexities of motherhood, particularly in the context of a child born from an illicit relationship. She stands as a bridge between past losses and the uncertain future of Thoithoi. Ekashini, depicted in the background holding Thoithoi as she prepares to leave, emerges as a figure of hope and redemption. Her actions represent a transformative potential; as Thoithoi's rightful caregiver, she seeks to make amends for her husband's past sins. By taking on the responsibility of raising an 'illegal' child, Ekashini not only attempts to reshape Thoithoi's future but also to confront the stigma surrounding their existence. Her presence in the background suggests she is both a hopeful influence and a counterpoint to Dinachandra's dishonour.

The grandfather, on seeing the mother-son bond, cries and leaves. The film ends with Ekashini correcting a step of the Thoithoi's Krishna dance, showing her love for her son, her precious. This scene, characterised by the delicate correction of a Krishna dance step, works as a powerful visual metaphor. Ekashini's face, illuminated by an expression of profound affection, surpasses the conventional bonds of familial relation. With a freeze-frame taking the tender moment of Ekashini lovingly cupping Thoithoi's cheeks as he plays the flute, this powerful image symbolizes their enduring emotional connection, suggesting that Ekashini's heart will forever be intertwined with that of her son.

The film's narrative is characterized by an examination of the human condition, as evident in the words of Aribam Syam Sharma, "In my films, there are no bad characters. Human beings are not bad, but it's the circumstance that makes man bad" (personal communication. 2021). This perspective is reflective of the filmmaker's intention to subvert conventional notions of morality.

One particularly noteworthy example of this complex portrayal is that of Ekashini, Dinachanda Sinam's wife. Initially, she is introduced as a figure who is distant and unemotional, but as the story progresses, her character evolves, and she develops a deep sense of maternal affection for Thoithoi, the child born out of her husband's illicit relationship. This transformation is a powerful commentary on the societal expectations of women and the ways in which they are often expected to conform to traditional roles. As Aribam Syam Sharma notes, "When I was in Santiniketan, we were taught that human beings cannot be as bad person by birth" (personal communication, 2021). This philosophical perspective is reflected in the film's narrative, which suggests that human behaviour is shaped by a complex interplay of circumstances, emotions, and relationships.

Pabung reflects on the profound impact of his work during a screening in New York. Following the film, an interaction session unfolded where the audience, predominantly women, engaged in a spirited dialogue. Many attendees expressed their surprise at the portrayal of the stepmother in the film, traditionally a role associated with villainy in many narratives. However, as Aribam notes, in *Imagi Ningthem*, the stepmother is depicted as a nurturing and caring figure, illustrating a significant departure from conventional storytelling. This prompted discussion among the viewers, who found it challenging to reconcile such a portrayal with their cultural perceptions. The willingness of the audience to engage in these discussions suggests a progressive shift toward understanding multifaceted perspectives on familial relationships, particularly the often-stigmatized role of the stepmother. Aribam recounts a memorable incident from the London Film Festival, further emphasizing the film's impact beyond the screen. After a morning screening, he proceeded to the cash counter for lunch where a Black student, recognizing him as the director of *Imagi Ningthem*, insisted on paying for his meal. The student, a member of the London Film School community, articulated that watching the film resonated with him profoundly, leading him to extend this gesture of kindness (personal communication, 2016). This moment, though seemingly modest, underscores the ripple effects of cinematic narratives, connecting individuals across cultural and geographical divides. The significance of such gestures cannot be overstated. In an era where the arts increasingly serve as a conduit for empathy and shared human experiences, Aribam's work exemplifies how cinema can bridge divides, provoke thought, and foster connections.

The film's reception is a testament to the power of cinematic storytelling to challenge societal norms and expectations. Initially, the film received negative responses from the audience in Manipur, with many producers criticizing Aribam for making a film that was deemed too radical and unconventional. However, the film's subsequent success at international film festivals, including the Grand Prix at the Festival of Three Continents, Nantes, and the Rajat Kamal for Best Regional Film at the 29th National Film Festival, 1982, served as a vindication of Aribam's artistic vision. As the filmmaker reminisces about his experiences with Adoor Gopalakrishnan, a renowned Indian filmmaker, it becomes clear that the non-conformist spirit of *Imagi Ningthem* was not an isolated phenomenon, but rather part of a larger movement in Indian cinema to challenge conventional narrative structures and explore new modes of storytelling. Aribam's comments on his interactions with Adoor Gopalakrishnan, "Adoor Gopalakrishnan and myself travelled together to London Film Festival... We came back together to India. He got recognition from BFI, and I from France" (Aribam, as quoted by the author), highlight the sense of camaraderie and shared purpose that exists among filmmakers who are committed to pushing the boundaries of cinematic storytelling.

Imagi Ningthem is a powerful and poignant film that offers a nuanced exploration of the human condition, challenging conventional societal norms and expectations. Through its thoughtful and empathetic portrayal of characters, the film presents a compelling commentary on the complexities of human relationships and the ways in which they are shaped by circumstance, emotion, and relationship. As Pabung's comments suggest, the film's narrative is characterized by a deep sense of philosophical and emotional insight, making it a significant contribution to the canon of Indian cinema.

Raghavendra (2009, p. 231) states, "The 'politicized' reading of *Imagi Ningthem* just advanced may not find favour with the viewer distracted by the film's humanity and its charm. *Imagi Ningthem* nevertheless distinctly posits two separate spaces, the village and the capital city, Imphal. The denizen of the city who enters the village arrives triumphantly like a victor but the inhabitant of the village who enters the city, arrives and departs like a supplicant. What is particularly interesting is the association made between the space of the city and the privilege it is bestowed. Aribam Syam Sharma lives in Imphal and we presume that it is not the relationship between his city and its surroundings with which his film is actually preoccupied. *Imagi Ningthem* is, perhaps, really about the privilege and authority that Delhi breeds in Manipur because bureaucrat in the provinces is a favoured representative of the centre. If the authority represented in Syam Sharma's film is benign, this benignity perhaps also reflects the helplessness of those who are at the mercy of its dispensations."

Raghavendra's analysis of Aribam's *Imagi Ningthem* (2009) offers a compelling, politicized interpretation that moves beyond the film's immediate aesthetic appeal. He argues that the film, despite its apparent humanism and charm, subtly delineates a power dynamic through its spatial representation of the village and the capital city, Imphal. This division is not merely geographical; it is intrinsically linked to social and political power. Raghavendra highlights the contrasting experiences of individuals moving between these spaces. The city dweller's entry into the village is portrayed as a triumphant arrival, reminiscent of a victor's procession. Conversely, the villager's journey to the city is marked by supplication and dependence. The core of Raghavendra's argument posits that *Imagi Ningthem* isn't primarily concerned with the local dynamic between Imphal and its surrounding villages. Instead, he suggests that the film subtly critiques the influence and authority wielded by Delhi in Manipur. He sees the bureaucrat figure in the film as a representative of the central government, embodying the power that Delhi bestows upon its representatives in the provinces. The film becomes an allegory for the relationship between the centre and the periphery, with Delhi representing the centre of power and Manipur occupying a subordinate position.

Raghavendra addresses the film's portrayal of authority as "benign." He suggests that this benignity might also reflect the vulnerability and dependence of those subject to the authority's decisions. The film, therefore, doesn't simply celebrate authority; it subtly acknowledges the power imbalance and the potential for those at the periphery to be at the "mercy of its dispensations." Raghavendra encourages a critical engagement with *Imagi Ningthem*, urging viewers to look beyond its surface charm and consider its underlying commentary on political power and regional disparity.

The opinions expressed by Derek Malcolm and another film critics and authors regarding Aribam's *Imagi Ningthem* (My Son, My Precious) open a rich discourse on the intersections of film technology, cultural representation, and the authenticity of storytelling in cinema. Malcolm's critique, loaded with both admiration and a critical eye, underscores a fundamental tension within the realm of art: the often-dichotomous relationship between technical execution and narrative depth.

Malcolm candidly acknowledges the film's technical limitations, remarking that it appeared as though "the film stock looked as if it was reconstituted waste paper" and noting the flickering images that invoke a sense of self-consciousness in their presentation. This assessment highlights how technological inadequacies can create a dissonance for audiences accustomed to the high production values often found in Western cinema. Yet, Malcolm's critique pivots dramatically when he emphasizes that these flaws do not detract from the film's broader narrative significance. He asserts, "Yet, the film... seemed to mean something quite apart from its technical deficiencies and the exigencies of its simple plot line." This underscores a vital point: that cinema can—and often does—transcend its material conditions to convey profound truths about human experience and cultural identity.

The film's focus on "real people," as opposed to "invented people," reinforces its connection to the lived experiences of individuals in India, rather than a fabricated representation of an exoticized East that often permeates Western narratives. Through this lens, *Imagi Ningthem* emerges not just as a cinematic experience but also as a cultural document that conveys the richness of Manipuri life, something that resonates particularly in a global context increasingly attentive to diverse narratives. Malcolm's statement about the film expressing "something true and honorable and exciting" captures the essence of cinema's potential to reflect genuine human conditions, irrespective of its technical polish.

Patricia Moraz's remarks further consolidate this perspective. By describing *Imagi Ningthem* as a work of art that "shows us things" and "makes us see," she elevates the film's ability to reveal deeper truths and evoke emotional responses beyond superficial entertainment value. This notion supports closely with the principles of neorealism, wherein the authenticity of storytelling often lies in the representation of everyday life, marked by its inherent challenges and imperfections rather than grand narratives.

Laifungbam Somi Roy's characterization of the film as "the first serious, non-formula film in Manipur" draws attention to its departure from conventional storytelling moulds that dominate both regional and global cinema. This assertion not only celebrates *Imagi Ningthem* for its artistic bravery but also serves as a catalyst for future filmmakers in Manipur and beyond. It suggests a need to embrace personal narratives that reflect local realities rather than adhering strictly to formulaic approaches that may fail to capture the complexities of the human experience.

M.K. Binodini shares her experience of screening the film in Kolkata just before it received an invitation to Nantes. In the documentary *Aribam Syam Sharma*, directed by Gurumayum Nirmal Sharma, she recalls that when the film was completed, they received an invitation from the film festival in Kolkata. Just before their film was set to screen, Aparna Sen's film, *36 Chowringhee Lane*, was shown. The auditorium was full, and the audience looked beautiful. We watched the film, but when it was our turn, we discovered that only 5 or 6 people, including some from Kolkata, were in attendance. I still remember that Manjushree Sarkar was with me; I had invited her. It was disheartening to see almost no audience in the auditorium when our film was being screened. We felt so small and dejected in that empty space.

Binodini's recollection of her experience screening the film in Kolkata offers a poignant commentary on the dynamics of acceptance and recognition within the film industry, particularly for regional and independent filmmakers. The feelings of marginalization and dejection expressed by Binodini are emblematic of a broader sentiment experienced by many independent filmmakers.

The discourse surrounding *Imagi Ningthem* reflects a remarkable intersection of technical critique and cultural appreciation. The film challenges audiences to reconsider their assumptions about the relationship between form and content in cinema. It emphasizes that the emotional and cultural resonance of a film can often outweigh its technological limitations, presenting an authentic narrative that is intricately tied to the real experiences of its subjects. Through this lens, *Imagi Ningthem* stands as a testament to the idea that greatness in cinema lies not solely in technical excellence, but in its capacity to connect with and authentically represent the diverse tapestry of human life.

A Turning Point after *Imagi Ningthem*

Interestingly, after *Imagi Ningthem*, Pabung Aribam stopped making films produced by private producers. Another significant milestone in his life was after *Ishanou* in 1991, when he resigned from his job as a lecturer. Pabung shares:

"It was a very important moment in my life: after *Imagi Ningthem*, I never made films produced by private producers. Moreover, after *Ishanou* in 1991, I gave up my job as a lecturer to become a full-fledged filmmaker. You know, in 1980, I made the film *Olangthagee Wangmadasoo*. It was a super hit and very popular among the local people. At the same time, it won Best Feature Film in Manipuri at the 27th National Film Awards. The producer, G. Narayan Sharma, was very happy with the enormous success of the film. The script was written by Maharaj Kumari Binodini specifically for the film, whereas *Imagi Ningthem* was originally a radio play and not written for film.

However, at the first screening of *Imagi Ningthem*, the theatre was not house full, and the film was not well received. In a sense, it was a disaster. The producer was not a wealthy man; he had taken loans from friends and others to complete the film. This situation pained me deeply. The public blamed me, as my previous film, *Olangthagee Wangmadasoo*, had been a huge success and brought financial benefits to its producer. But with *Imagi Ningthem*, the producer did not make money from the theatre, nor did the film receive a positive public response. People even criticized me. But, the producer, K. Ibohal Sharma, was a good man, but the situation made his family unhappy. I felt very sorry for the entire situation. After the first week of screening, it became very difficult to keep the film running due to a lack of audience, and the theatre owner did not want to continue showing it. I was so disappointed that I thought it was time to say goodbye to filmmaking."

Imagi Ningthem was later selected for the Indian Panorama, which was part of the Calcutta Filmotsav in January 1982. Despite receiving an invitation, Pabung did not attend the festival, nor did he attend the National Award ceremony. However, he received an invitation from New York to screen the film in the "New Directors, New Films" segment. The festival officials mentioned that they would not screen the film without the filmmaker's presence. For the sake of Manipuri cinema, the producer K. Ibohal Sharma and Pabung decided to attend. Despite this, Pabung kept his promise not to make films produced by private producers, and only agreed to make films financed by the Government of India or other government departments, as those losses did not matter as much. He also stopped making films for G. Narayan Sharma. Since then, Pabung did not make any films for private producers, despite receiving many requests, except for those financed by the Indian or Manipuri State Government.

Ishanou: A Visual Poem

Pabung Aribam's film *Ishanou* (The Chosen One) represents a pivotal moment in the landscape of Manipuri cinema and Indian cinema at large. The film's selection for the Un Certain Regard category at the Cannes Film Festival in 1991 and London Film Festival not only focuses its artistic merit but also shows the cultural narratives and themes that permeate the film. It expresses the often underrepresented voices within Indian cinema. On the webpage of the Academy Museum of Motion Pictures, it states, "*Ishanou* is a poignant tale of love and loss steeped in Manipuri culture that tells the story of Tampha (Anoubam Kiranmala), who abandons her husband and daughter to join the Maibi sect of priestesses. But behind her absorption into the mystical world of the Maibis lurks the anguish of a mother alienated from her child. The film beautifully juxtaposes the spiritual world of the Maibis with the rhythm of ordinary life. The simplicity of the director's approach, delicate camerawork, and understated acting, combined with the vivid depiction of the Maibi culture and use of the traditional music of Manipur, gives the film an authenticity that blends storytelling, documentary, and ethnography" (Academy Museum of Motion Pictures, 2025).

In the opening scene of the film, we are introduced to Khongjom Bazaar, where a city bus comes to a stop. Dhanabir, Tampha, and their daughter Bembem disembark and make their way to Angoubi's stall, which is run by Tampha's mother, a 50-year-old widow. The scene then shifts from the mandap of a temple to Angoubi's house and then to a nearby tank, where Tampha is seen fishing with a net, accompanied by several young women. As she prepares to draw in the net, Dhanabir playfully approaches her from behind and tugs at it, startling Tampha and causing her to drop the net. After a brief exchange of light-hearted conversation, they walk home together from the tank. While they are walking, Dhanabir shares some exciting news: "Remember the scooter I was talking about? Well, I found one in good condition! The owner is selling it due to an emergency and has priced it at ten thousand. Of course, we can negotiate a couple of thousand here and there, but he needs the money within two weeks." As the story unfolds, we later see that they have successfully purchased the scooter. In a quick passing shot, Dhanabir, Tampha, and Bembem can be seen riding away on it, which symbolizes a new chapter in their lives.

Tampha is a joyful life in the Manipur valley with her devoted husband and daughter. Every day, she is preoccupied with everyday things like preparing for her daughter's ear-piercing ceremony and considering the idea of buying a second hand scooter with her husband. Everything seems normal, and the family enjoys wonderful times together.

The narrative of the film begins with a liner structure, presenting a clear and simple storyline that is easy for the audience to follow. However, the film transforms from a simple depiction of everyday life into a richer and more layered exploration of human experiences. Subtle nuances begin to emerge, revealing the characters' inner struggles, aspirations, and the societal challenges they face. The initial light-heartedness of the film contrasts with underlying tensions.

A significant moment occurs when Tampha and her husband are seen riding their scooter, eventually stopping near a hillock to explore the area. As they begin to climb, Tampha takes a moment to look around. Her gaze lands on a tree from which clusters of blue Vanda orchids dangle gracefully. Suddenly, she notices a small flower within the bunch gently swaying as if it is calling out to her. Softly, and unheard by her husband, she muses, "That flower is calling me! I wonder why." Intrigued, she approaches the flower, plucks it, and tucks it behind her ear, singing a little tune as she does so. Dhanabir, finding her actions amusing, hugs her. However, at that moment, Tampha suddenly begins to feel unwell, leaning against him. This marks the first hint, as suggested by the filmmaker, that she may be under the influence of some divine power.

Again when she sees the catfish in the kitchen, her sudden behavioural change, marks a turning point in the narrative. She begins conversing with the flowers as if they can hear her, growing lightheaded and disoriented. One night, she leaves the house without telling anyone. In one scene, Dhanabir and Tampha are asleep when Tampha stirs awake. With a dreamy smile, she rises and quietly steps outside. In the darkness, she makes her way to a nearby hillock. Dhanabir wakes to find her gone and, worried, searches for her. He soon discovers her playfully running around a tree, caught up in a game of hide-and-seek. Her strange behaviour concerns her family, who grow anxious for her well-being. Loving and supportive, her family starts a journey to find a solution to her mysterious symptoms. They visit different places, seeking help from various people, hoping to understand what is happening to Tampha. After much searching, they come to a surprising realization: Tampha is not suffering from any illness. Instead, she is responding to a divine call from the gods, something that is beyond sickness and needs to be understood with a sense of spirituality and connection to higher powers.

Tampha's divine calling becomes intertwined with the spiritual fabric of Manipuri culture through the concept of the Maibi. The Maibi, or priestess, holds a significant place within Manipuri society, serving as a medium between the human realm and divine spirits. The film utilizes Tampha's uncanny transformation as both a plot device and a metaphor for larger existential themes such as the struggle between personal desires and communal responsibilities as well as the challenging experiences of motherhood. Aribam's portrayal of Tampha's journey reflects the complexities of a woman's role in a society where cultural expectations may often clash with individual aspirations.

The link between Tampha and the *ngakra* (catfish), functioning as a symbolic sign of her divine calling, shows the complex and sometimes mysterious nature of connections within Manipuri spiritual practice. The assertion that the Meibis cannot consume or even observe the *ngakra* presents a fascinating point of contention within the cultural frameworks and belief systems of the local community. This divinely ordained choice leaves Tampha's family grappling with her transformation, focusing on the ambiguous terrain between personal loss and cultural duty. Moreover, the emotional toll on Tampha, particularly in her separation from her daughter Bembem, serves to foreground the theme of maternal sacrifice. Pabung Aribam crafts a poignant narrative arc that resonates universally, elucidating the pain that accompanies profound change, especially when it compels a mother to reconcile her love for her family with a spiritual calling that propels her away from them. This tension is emblematic not only of Tampha's internal struggles but also reflects a broader commentary on the expectations placed upon women, often necessitating a choice between self-identity and familial attachment, a phenomenon that transcends cultural boundaries.

Regarding the music in this film, Pabung notes that *Ishanou*, in its dance sequence, incorporates the mandatory song and dance elements. For this reason, the music in other parts of the film needed to be minimal. I chose to adapt the folk tune "Pithadoi" as the thematic music for Thampa's recurring experiences. The high-pitched bamboo flute beautifully complements the visual effect in these scenes. The music accompanying the stark white titles over a black background features an incantation hymn of the Maiba, accompanied by the pena. This hymn focuses on creation (genesis) according to Meitei beliefs. Its symbolic nature and hypnotic quality set the stage for the unusual story that unfolds. The music used in the film is the traditional music of Manipur, the creators of which have long been forgotten over time, yet it has become a treasured part of Meitei culture. The song played in the background when the protagonist learns the truth about her baby's abduction acquires a different meaning in the context of the scene (Sharma, 2006, 59).

Pabung recalls his experience at the Hawai Film Festival, where, following the screening, he attended a dinner party. During the event, a woman approached him, visibly emotional. She expressed her profound gratitude, saying, "I am very happy to meet you." She shared a heart-breaking revelation: her elder sister had mirrored the tragic behaviour of Thompha, leaping from the seventh floor of a building to commit suicide. The woman lamented that if only the film had been seen earlier, perhaps her sister could have been saved through the transformative power of training, music, dance, love, and understanding. She emphasized that the film served as an eye-opener for them (personal communication, 2016).

The filmmaker's experience during the screening at the Hawai'i International Film Festival attests to the film's potent emotional resonance and its ability to provoke reflection on personal and societal complexities. The connection made between Tampha's narrative and the audience member's own tragic experiences aptly illustrates the film's broader implications about mental health, spirituality, and societal support systems, a vacationing moment that raises critical conversations about how society engages with such profoundly individual experiences.

Although *Ishanou* garnered accolades, including the Rajat Kamal for Best Regional Film (Best Feature Film in Each of the Language Other Than Those Specified in the Schedule VIII of the Constitution), his frustration with the reception of the film within India suggests the pervasive biases that may exist towards regional cinema. He was hurt when a Chennai-based journalist described it as a "Manipuri film" instead of saying it was "an Indian film." The filmmaker believes that since it was the only Indian entry at Cannes, it should be recognized as part of India as a whole, rather than just one region. He wanted everyone to celebrate it as a representation of India, stressing unity over regional differences. His desire for recognition as part of a unified Indian cinematic landscape, rather than a segregated regional entry, speaks to the aspirations of many filmmakers from diverse backgrounds seeking visibility and validation. This sentiment echoes a larger discourse about identity and representation within the Indian film industry, where films from smaller regions often fight preconceived notions and biases.

Ishanou is not merely a narrative about the transformation of a woman into a Maibi, but rather a rich scenario that explores the emotional and cultural depths of Manipuri society. The film invites audiences to delve into the complexities of belief, identity, and the struggles inherent in balancing personal desires with communal expectations. It stands as both a significant cultural work and a catalyst for important dialogues surrounding gender, spirituality, and the experience of women in navigating their roles within society.

The context surrounding Pabung's film *Ishanou* reveals not only the artistic significance of the film but also the socio-political dynamics that influence filmmaking in India, particularly in the North-Eastern region. Late Aruna Vasudev's account in *The Hindustan Times* (June 8, 1991) captures the challenges faced by the film. It states that despite *Ishanou* being recognized and invited to major film festivals like Singapore and Cannes, administrative hurdles posed by the Ministry of Information and Broadcasting reflect a larger narrative about how regional cinema often receives inadequate support from centralized governmental bodies. Notably, the Ministry's refusal to provide funding for the director's travel underscores a pervasive disconnect between the cultural importance of a film and bureaucratic recognition. Vasudev asserts, "Yet it was the only Indian film in the festival, and had been produced by Doordarshan." This statement indicates the film's historical and cultural significance as it represents not only the region of Manipur but also the burgeoning voice of Indian cinema on international platforms.

As *The Telegraph* (January 11, 1991) describes, the film represents a "definite departure" from Aribam's past works, such as *Lamja Parsuram*, *Saphabee*, and *Imagi Ningthem*. This suggests a deliberate evolution in Aribam's filmmaking, moving from narratives deeply rooted in Manipuri culture and class consciousness to exploring more universal themes and emotional landscapes. John Warrington's description of *Ishanou* as a "festival masterpiece" and a "poem on celluloid" encapsulates not just the aesthetic qualities of the film but elevates it to a form of high art. It implies that *Ishanou* transcends conventional storytelling to convey deeper philosophical and emotional truths, effectively blurring the lines between visual art and cinema. This characterization encourages a perception of the film as a significant cultural work, deserving recognition and study within the global cinematic canon.

Moreover, David Overby's observation that *Ishanou* addresses themes that are essentially "exotic even for Indian audiences" while also presenting "emotional situations (that) are universal," explains the dual nature of regional cinema. By presenting culturally specific narratives that still touch upon universal human experiences—such as love, loss, and identity—Aribam allows *Ishanou* to act as a bridge between local and global narratives.

David Stratton writes in *Variety*, dated March 11, 1991, that "scenes of religious dances in the second part of the film could be slightly trimmed, but otherwise this unsettling, visually beautiful film should be well received by Western audiences. It's technically fine, apart from slightly washed-out colour." Stratton shows the potential challenges and attractions of the film for a Western audience. Stratton notes that some scenes, particularly those featuring "religious dances in the second part of the film," might be slightly too prolonged or excessive for Western viewers. He cautions that these sequences may overwhelm or alienate some audience members due to their unfamiliarity or cultural detachment from such customs. Conversely, Stratton emphasizes the film's potential to captivate and unsettle Western viewers, particularly through its "visually beautiful" and thought-provoking portrayal of cultural clashes. Stratton's assessment suggests that Western audiences may be drawn to the film's striking visuals, but may struggle with some of its pacing and thematic elements, particularly those rooted in cultural specificity.

The film *Ishanou* signifies not just a cinematic achievement but also represents the struggles of regional filmmakers within a national framework that often overlooks their contributions. The film's journey—from its bureaucratic challenges to its exalted position in international film festivals—reflects the tension between cultural expression and institutional support. The accolades it received serve not only as a testament to Aribam's skill but also as a call for greater acknowledgment and support of regional voices in the broader Indian film industry. As regional cinemas continue to emerge and assert their identities within the global landscape, the narrative of *Ishanou* stands as an instructive example of both the hurdles to be overcome and the triumphs that can ensue.

Restored version of *Ishanou*

Shivendra Singh Dungarpur, founder director of Film Heritage Foundation, writes that the first time he saw *Ishanou* was in April 2021 when he was in Imphal, Manipur, with the Film Heritage Foundation team for a special project: helping the Manipur government set up a film archive. One evening in Imphal, he attended a screening of *Ishanou.* He was excited because they were screening a 35mm print of the film, which has become such a rarity these days. He also had the privilege of meeting the director, Aribam Syam Sharma, a doyen of Manipuri cinema and a Renaissance man.

When the film began, he could see that the print was not in the best condition, with scratches, flicker, and uneven colors that disturbed the eye. Yet the beauty of the film, and the simple but powerful narrative rooted in the unique culture of Manipur, transcended the distortions that marred the artistry of the imagery playing out on the big screen. He was mesmerized by the poignancy of the story of a young mother torn between her family and the call of the divine. He was determined that *Ishanou* must be restored to its former glory and that the world should be reminded of a filmmaker who had put Manipuri cinema on the world map (Film Heritage Foundation, 2024).

In 2023, the prestigious 76th Cannes Film Festival marked a significant moment by presenting the restored version of *Ishanou.* Screened on May 19th within the esteemed Cannes Classics program, a showcase of globally significant cinematic achievements, the film was selected for its artistic qualities from a competitive field of 150 submissions. The restoration, a project undertaken by the Film Heritage Foundation (FHF) in partnership with the Manipur State Film Development Society that same year, highlights the film's enduring significance. While Aribam could not attend due to health issues, his presence was honored by the attendance of lead actor Kangabam Tomba Singh and film preservationist Shivendra Singh Dungarpur, underscoring the collective commitment to cinematic heritage and artistic expression.

Amidst the traumatic, communal crisis that Manipur is currently going through, a Manipuri feature film by Aribam Syam Sharma, *Ishanou* has be recognized as World Classic ("Manipuri Feature Film *ISHANOU* Recognised as World Classic," 2023). The recognition of his *Ishanou* as a World Classic arrives at a poignant and complex moment for Manipur. While the state grapples with a deeply traumatic communal crisis, this cinematic honour provides a glimmer of cultural pride and a reminder of the region's artistic heritage. The timing is crucial, contrasting sharply with the ongoing turmoil in Manipur, suggesting the spirit of Manipuri culture and its enduring value, even amidst immense suffering. As a film recognized as a "World Classic," *Ishanou* transcends its status as mere film, but represents Manipuri society, traditions, and artistic expression.

In a groundbreaking moment for Manipuri cinema, the Academy Museum of Motion Pictures in Los Angeles has announced the screening of *Ishanou* on March 11, as part of the film series "Emotion in Colour: A Kaleidoscope of Indian Cinema," which runs from March 7 to April 19, 2025. Curated by renowned filmmaker and preservationist Shivendra Singh Dungarpur, this historic series highlights 12 iconic Indian films, examining the evolution of colour in Indian cinema and its influence on storytelling and visual artistry. The line-up includes cinematic masterpieces such as *Mother India* (1957), *Manthan* (1976), *Amar Akbar Anthony* (1977), *Mirch Masala* (1987), *Devdas* (2002), *Dilwale Dulhania Le Jayenge* (1995), *Jodhaa Akbar* (2008), *Kanchenjungha* (1962), *Maya Darpan* (1972), *Iruvar* (1997), and *Kummatty* (1997), with *Ishanou* (1990) representing Manipuri cinema on this prestigious global platform. (*Academy Museum in Los Angeles to Showcase Ishanou 20250223*, 2025).

The recognition of *Ishanou* also brings international attention to Manipuri cinema and, by extension, to Manipur itself, potentially leading to greater awareness of the crisis and generating support for peace and reconciliation efforts.

Aribam Syam Sharma's two films, *Imagi Ningthem* (1981) and *Ishanou* (1990), primarily reshaped Manipuri cinema, uplifting its visibility on the global stage and setting its distinct cultural identity. These seminal films have not only redefined the landscape of Manipuri cinema but have also contributed significantly to broader scholarly discourse on regional identities within the global cinematic landscape.

***

Works Cited

Academy Museum of Motion Pictures. (n.d.). *Ishanou.* https://www.academymuseum.org/en/programs/detail/ishanou-019475ce-004d-f999-e4da-5bf3e217835f

Academy Museum in Los Angeles to showcase Ishanou 20250223. (2025).https://epao.net/epSubPageExtractor.asp?src=announcements.Ann_2025.Academy_Museum_in_Los_Angeles_to_showcase_Ishanou_20250223

Film Heritage Foundation's restoration of Aribam Syam Sharma's film *Ishanou* (1990, Manipur) selected for world premiere at Cannes Film Festival 2023. https://filmheritagefoundation.co.in/ishanou-1990-restoration-project/

Manipuri feature film 'ISHANOU' recognised as World Classic. (2023, May 6). *The Economic Times.*

https://economictimes.indiatimes.com/news/india/manipuri-feature-film-ishanou-recognised-as-world-classic/articleshow/100038686.cms?from=mdr

Overby, D. (1991). Review of *Ishanou. Contemporary World Cinema*

Raghavendra, M. K. (2009). *50 Indian film classics.* HarperCollins.

Sharma, A. S. (2006). *Living shadows.* Gauhati Cine Club. Guwahati, Assam.

The Telegraph. (1991, January 11). Film Review: *Ishanou*

Vasudev, A. (1991, June 8). Film Review: *Ishanou. The Hindustan Times*

Warrington, J. (1991). Review of *Ishanou.* BBC correspondent, *The Guardian*

Chapter Five

Voice from Shadows

Many of Pabung Aribam's films, be they feature or non-feature films, are still unknown, although some have won praise from critics and gained widespread recognition. This chapter throws light on these films that show his extraordinary knack for keeping the spirit of Manipuri culture. Pabung develops stories that have a strong emotional impact on audiences by heavily drawing from social issues, folklore and conflicts between tradition and modernity. His lesser-known films, which illustrate the intricacies of the Manipuri way of life through colourful landscapes, unique customs, and a deep connection to nature, dwell mainly on the complexities of human emotions. It introduces us to the rich cultural diversity and lived experiences of Manipuri society, a region that is frequently marginalised in film discussions. Pabung's non-feature films, which are akin to visual and lyrical poems on screen, are also the subject of this chapter. These films encourage us to look at the less well-known but extremely significant parts of the wide world of films. These films use poetic storytelling and striking visuals to inspire contemporary audiences to look for and appreciate the hidden gems that often go unnoticed.

Pabung's fifth film, *Paokhum Ama* (The Only Answer, 1983), was scripted by M.K. Binodini and made in two languages– Meitei and Tangkhul. It is a political film that subtly addresses the stark realities of Manipur, including rampant unemployment and the growing disillusionment among youth regarding governmental policies. It explores the difficulties families face when they try to find their children stable government jobs, only to have their efforts repeatedly derailed by systemic corruption. The story effectively illustrates how these frustrations can lead to radicalisation and armed resistance among young people in Manipur. The film also precisely examines the complex relationship between Manipur's hills and valleys that shows the region's distinct socio-political landscape and the challenges that arise from its diverse communities.

Pabung writes in his book *Living Shadows*, "Since it was a proposal to the Film Division, the script had to be socially relevant; it had to possess 'redeeming values.' The script, written by Sanaibemma (M.K. Binodini), weaves into its fabric the problems faced in Manipur during that period, issues which are still there now. The reality of corruption, the cultural divide between the hill and the valley that could not be bridged, and slight references to the origins and motivations of insurgency were the undercurrents of the film." Once, noted film critic Samik Banerjee told Pabung that Aribam was the only director who took money from the government to criticize it, as Pabung writes in the book.

The film shows the shift of the youth's mind set in the Manipuri society from seeking government job to the self-reliance through the protagonist of the film Iboyaima. In this society, the search for employment is a pressing concern—almost everyone is eager, if not desperate, to secure a job. When Iboyaima's family received news from a Maibi Laiphao, through his Eteima, that he would soon get a job, there was a palpable sense of relief and happiness within the household. Believing that a little help could guarantee the opportunity, his Eteima and elder brother decided to offer money to Ta Gouro, an associate of a government minister, hoping to secure the position for Iboyaima. Unfortunately, their hopes were dashed when the job was instead given to someone who could pay a higher bribe. This disappointment underscored the harsh reality of the pervasive corruption and the challenges faced by ordinary families seeking government employment.

Meanwhile, Ta Ngou, a teacher from Ukhrul and a settler, extended an invitation to Iboyaima and his journalist friend Birchandra to come and teach in Ukhrul. Iboyaima accepted the offer, but Birchandra did not join him—having published a controversial news report, Birchandra was compelled to move far away from the region for his own safety. Upon arriving in Ukhrul, Iboyaima met Hermi, Ta Ngou's sister-in-law. There was an undeniable chemistry between the two, yet neither found the courage to acknowledge their feelings. Alone but undeterred, Iboyaima journeyed to Ukhrul, unaware that this new chapter would lead him to Hermi, Ta Ngou's charming sister-in-law. (Here, I would like to focus on the fact that the Tangkhul Nagas live in the lovely hill district of Ukhrul in Manipur. The film brilliantly depicts the yearning resulting from the growing gap separating Manipur's hills from valleys. Though their historical and cultural presence is firmly ingrained in the Meitei consciousness, the Tangkhuls have long led front stage in the Naga Movement in the Northeast. In one of the Meitei origin tales, the Tangkhul Nagas are even revered as elder brothers, pointing out the strong and long-lasting ties between the two societies.)

As time went by, societal expectations prevailed: Hermi's elders arranged her marriage to a local Ukhrul boy. Iboyaima, heartbroken and speechless, could do nothing but witness the union from afar. Their mutual affection remained unspoken, existing only in fleeting, imagined moments, a love that blossomed in a world of fantasy but never manifested in reality. Eventually, Iboyaima returned to the Valley to reunite with his family as his younger brother, who had just completed his studies in agriculture, came home. This time, Iboyaima felt empowered; with his brother's expertise, he saw the potential to improve their family farm, aiming to apply modern agricultural knowledge to boost both the quality and quantity of their produce. No longer dependent on elusive government jobs, Iboyaima found new hope in building a sustainable and prosperous future through agriculture. Kongbram (2021) states that the film exposes the various social issues on unemployment, corruption and insurgency which were prevalent in the society. Besides, it explores the healthy and strong relationship between the Vaishnavite Meities living in the plains and the Christian tribals in the hills of Manipur with sincerity and conviction. The film was screened in the UK in 1984 (p.79).

Pabung shares an intriguing anecdote in his book: "Ukhrul, where the major part of the film was shot, is a lovely part of the Manipuri hills. At the present times, we would perhaps not get the friendly and warm assistance that we got during the making of the film. Certain images from real life crept into the film unconsciously. The shot where the heroine and the hero take a climb together was specifically taken to insert wonderful cloud-laden hills that I saw during a morning walk with my little son during our stay in Ukhrul. Later, someone, after seeing the film, pointed out that it was not a very rare thing in Ukhrul. He said it was very common. I did not know whether to feel sorry for him or to thank him for pointing it out as an 'ordinary' thing (p.62).

The lead actress of the film, Yengkhum Roma, explains, "Pabung Aribam never tells us to imitate him. Instead, he explains the scenes and articulates what he expects from us. He then encourages us to express our feelings within the context of his guidance. This approach puts the artists at ease and allows them to perform effectively" (Aribam Syam Sharma, dir. by Gurumayum Nirmal Sharma).

His seventh film *Sanabi* (The Grey Mare,1995), script by M.K. Binodini and produced by Doordarshan and National Film Development Corporation (NFDC), was adapted from Binodini's short story *Sagol Sanabi.* It is about a dancer Sakhi, her childhood friend Mangi and a beautiful grey mare-Sanabi. The film tells the story of Sakhi, a beautiful dancer, and Mangi, *Shaning hanba* (cattle-rustler) who loves her. The tale begins when Sakhi, recently divorced, returns to her father's home. Her father, Ojha Birchandra, owns Sanabi, a stunning grey mare. Mangi, who has loved Sakhi since childhood, comes to visit her, but she initially ignores him. As the story unfolds, we see Sakhi perform various classical dances, showcasing her talent and passion for the art. Mangi, hoping to get Sakhi's attention, makes a bold move by stealing Sanabi, her beloved horse. This act is a mix of desperation and love, as he believes that taking something precious to her might help rekindle their connection. Eventually, Mangi realizes that his actions were wrong and returns Sanabi. This act of returning the horse symbolizes his change and willingness to do what is right.

Pabung Aribam explains in his book *Living Shadows* that the original story revolves around a horse-hustler's love for a woman and how he uses his profession as a thief to express his feelings to her, not through words, but through unambiguous actions. He keeps this plot intact but adds a parallel theme based on the Sagol or Manipuri pony, which is a vital prop of the original story. To him, the Sagol symbolises tradition and serves as a metaphor for the threat of the obliteration of identity. Since the introduction of Arabian Horses by the Allied forces during the Second World War, breeding or caring for the native pony has stopped, resulting in only crossbreeds between these horses today. The film partly raises the question of if the pony were to disappear from the planet, how close people are to facing the same fate. The attempt is to broach this subject as an undertone to the original story (p.63).

The film won Best Feature Film in Manipuri at the 43rd National Film Awards and was selected at the Cairo International Film Festival, Egypt, 1996. It won V. Shantaram Award for Best Direction in 1997.

Pabung takes up Thang-ta, the indigenous Manipuri martial art and HIV menace as the theme of his short feature film *Shingnaba* (Challenge, 1998), produced by Film Division, India. The story and screenplay of the film was written by Lamabam Birmani, a renowned short story writer from Manipur. Birmani received the Sahitya Akademi Award in 1984 for his highly acclaimed second book, *Chekla Paikhrabada* (1981). His literary achievements continued with the Jamini Sundar Guha Gold Medal for *Ukhruldei* (1998) and the prestigious Katha Award for *Rath Jatra* in 2000.

The film presents Ipu, a grandmaster of Thang-ta, who embodies the essence of dedication and the transmission of cultural heritage through martial arts. Thang-ta, an indigenous Manipuri martial art, is not merely a physical discipline but a profound cultural expression that integrates philosophy, history, and spirituality. Ipu's commitment extends beyond his individual prowess; he aspires to imbue his grandchildren, Thambal and Mani, with the same ardour for Thang-ta, observing it as a medium for infusing resilience and strength. Bikram, a student of Thang-ta, arrives from Silchar to learn from Ipu. As Ipu mentors Bikram, he simultaneously deals with the generational shifts and societal changes that impact his family, particularly Thambal's life course. Her marriage to a boy from Imphal initially promises familial expansion and continuity; however, this dream is shattered by tragedy as she is thrust into the grim realities of loss and disease. She became a widow after her husband sudden death. Not long after, it was discovered she was suffering from AIDS. Unknowingly, the innocent Thambal had contracted disease from her husband who happened to be a drug addict. The sudden death of her husband, compounded by the revelation of her AIDS diagnosis, poignantly analyses the weaknesses that intersect with social stigma and health crises. Destined to die, Ipu urged her to confront life with courage, like a true martial artist. Ipu's response to Thambal's plight embodies the philosophical foundations of martial arts—courage in the face of adversity. He employs his role as a grandmaster not only to impart physical skills but to teach life's difficult lessons: the importance of facing one's challenges with valour, akin to the mental and emotional fortitude required in martial arts.

Pabung Aribam was drawn to Lamabam's story because it was an opportunity to reflect on themes such as resilience, defeat, and courage. Throughout his films, he often contemplates the notion of a "martial race"—in this context, the Meitei people—and examines how such a community responds to adversity, particularly recalling their defeat by the British in 1891. This historical loss gave rise to a distinctive musical tradition: a balladic style of singing called as "Khongjom Parva" that is said to have originated with Samjetsabam Leinou, popularly known as Dhobi Leinou. It is said that Dhobi Leinou travelled from village to village, sharing firsthand accounts of the the valour and sacrifices of Manipuri soldiers who fought against the British Empire in the events of the Anglo-Manipur War of 1891. It seems that Pabung Aribam, in his own way, wished to capture something of this spirit in his film. The narrative also subtly acknowledges the significant challenges that Manipur faced during the peak of the HIV/AIDS epidemic, adroitly intertwining past and present struggles in a thoughtful and poignant manner.

It may be mentioned here that Pabung Aribam directed and produced the documentary *Mr Manipur* (2008), which offers a poignant and sensitive portrayal of Khundrakpam Pradipkumar, a 40-year-old bodybuilder from Manipur who is living with HIV. Using Pabung's unique cinematic vision, he explores Pradipkumar's inspirational journey, focusing on his tenacity and will against prejudice and hardship. The documentary not only follows Pradipkumar's personal challenges and victories but also shows broader social issues surrounding HIV/AIDS in the region. The documentary was screened at the MIAAC Film Festival in New York in November 2008. In the documentary, Pabung deftly guides and gently chronicles the narrative of Pradipkumar, who, despite being HIV-positive, accomplished the amazing feat of earning the *Mr. Manipur* title in the 60 kg category. The documentary is evidence of Pabung's dedication to sharing powerful, human-centred narratives that appeal far beyond Manipur's boundaries.

Paari (2000) produced by Children's Film Society of India, is a Children film. It is a dance drama that describes against the backdrop of Keibul Lamjao National Park. Sanathoi, a spirited young boy, eagerly embarks on an adventure with his friends and their enthusiastic teacher, who is passionate about wildlife conservation. As they journey through the lush landscapes, their excitement builds. However, the day's adventure takes a poignant turn when they stumble upon an injured Sangai fawn, the rare deer species. The sight of the struggling fawn profoundly affects Sanathoi. He feels a deep connection to this creature, sensing its pain and isolation. Later, filled with concern and compassion, he rushes home to share his feelings with his beloved grandfather, Idhou. Idhou spins enchanting tales about the Sangai and its significance within their landscape. His stories transport Sanathoi into a world where the Sangai roams freely. The tales of courage and survival stay deeply with him, inspiring vivid daydreams where he imagines himself as Paari, a brave guardian of the Sangai. In these fantasies, he imagines not only rescuing the injured fawn but also reuniting it with its family, weaving his own aspirations into the narrative of the wild. Sanathoi decides to embark on a quest to seek an audience with the Sangai king, a mythical figure he believes can help heal the fawn and restore balance to the forest. The journey through the jungle becomes a reflection of his inner thoughts and dreams, that expresses resilience and creativity of a child's mind.

The film beautifully illustrates the interplay of imagination and consciousness that defines childhood. As Sanathoi dances, he represents not just the physicality of the Sangai but also its spirit and plight. Sanathoi learns that even in a world filled with challenges, one can be a beacon of compassion and action. Through trials and transformations, Paari discovered that protecting nature meant preserving not just the environment but the bonds that connect them all. Years later, this film was showcased at the 12th International Children Film Festival of India.

His feature film *Leipaklei* (flower, 2012) was premiered on the opening day of the 5th Guwahati Film Festival in 2012. It was subsequently showcased at the 18th Kolkata International Film Festival and the Jeonju International Film Festival (JIFF) in Jeonju, South Korea in a special section called 'Beyond Bollywood'. The film received the National Film

Award for Best Feature Film in Manipuri at the 60th National Film Awards.

The story of *Leipaklei* revolves around a Manipuri woman named Leipaklei, who shares her name with a flower. The filmmaker draws a parallel between the flower and the woman, suggesting that both are surrounded by suffering. Leipaklei faces despair because she is separated from her husband (Her husband said to his wife that he would go to Makokching village, but he never returns) and must struggle to support herself and her young daughter. Much like the Leipaklei flower, which lies hidden and waiting for spring beneath the dry ground, she dreams of her husband's return. The film explores how the male gaze—society's way of looking at and judging women—adds to her struggles. Leipaklei's life is complicated by societal expectations about gender, making her feel undervalued. Her husband never returns but her teenage friend returns, which was a symbol of hope and the possibility of a better future. *Leipaklei* is not just a story about a woman's hardships; it also speaks to broader themes of resilience and hope. The connection between the woman and the flower suggests how, even in tough times, the human spirit can endure and aspire for renewal. National award winning Manipuri actress Leishangthem Tonthoingambi Devi, popularly known as Tonthoi who played the lead role in the film Leipaklei, Tonthoi says, "The character of Leipaklei was very challenging as it narrates the story of a woman who is surrounded by ill fates. She is depicted in the film as a symbol of patience and strength. Leipaklei is a local flower found in Manipur. Working with Pabung Aribam was an ultimate life-fulfilling experience (personal communication, April 30, 2016).

His latest film *Nongphadok Lakpa Atithi* (The Guest, 2019) represents a significant contribution to contemporary cinema, particularly in the context of Indian regional films. Directed by Pabung Aribam, this film was honored as the opening film at the 12th International Guwahati Film Festival in 2020. The film draws its narrative from the noted writer Lamabam Viramani's short story "Atithi," originally transformed into a radio play by M. K. Binodini Devi under the title *Nongphadok Lakpada*. The screenplay adaptation, written by Sharma, reflects an understanding of the source material, making this his 15th feature film. Produced by Doordarshan, with Deepak Sharma as the producer, the film has been recognized for its artistic merit, winning four awards at the 13th Manipur State Film Festival in 2020, including Best Director and Best Screenplay (Adapted). Such accolades prove the film's technical and narrative strengths, particularly in cinematography and audiography. The film's selection for the 5th North-East Film Festival in Pune show its cultural significance within the broader landscape of Indian cinema.

At the heart of the film lies an exploration of estrangement and reconciliation, expressed through the relationship between Tamubi and her estranged husband. The narrative unfolds against the backdrop of their twelve-year separation, with Tamubi initially resolute in her decision not to engage with her husband. However, familial obligations compel her to attend her daughter's wedding. Upon her arrival, the couple's silence becomes a powerful narrative device, indicating the weight of unresolved emotions and the complexities of their shared history. The ensuing night, spent under one roof, acts as a crucible for reflection and introspection, as both characters deal with their pasts and the choices that led them to this moment. The following day presents a pivotal moment; her husband's plea for reconciliation stands in stark contrast to Tamubi's steadfast commitment to her self-determination. This conflict shows broader themes of identity, agency, and the nuances of marital dynamics. It questions the nature of love, the implications of separation, and the struggle for personal integrity within relational frameworks.

The film *Nongphadok Lakpa Atithi* transcends its narrative to provoke critical reflection on the complexities of human connections, the passage of time, and the often insurmountable distances shaped by our choices.

Documentary Delights: Cultural Treasures

Pabung Aribam's documentaries are indispensable for ethnographic research and the preservation of culture. While he is widely known for his fiction feature films, his contributions to the documentary genre are equally significant. Each documentary is imbued with a profound understanding and representation of the socio-cultural landscape of North-East India. His documentaries are characterized by their meticulous attention to detail and a commitment to authenticity that capture the rich cultural traditions and practices of various indigenous communities of the region. By focusing on the Manipuri culture, he showcases the interplay of art forms such as dance and music, which are vital in understanding the region's identity. His documentaries deal with a wide variety of subjects ranging from Manipuri culture to the traditions of Mao Naga and Maram tribes, and the Monpas of Arunachal Pradesh.

In light of modernity and globalisation, Pabung's research on the Monpas of Arunachal Pradesh offers a chance to discuss issues of cultural sustainability and preservation. His films can be interpreted as interventions that challenge hegemonic narratives and advance a more inclusive view of India's cultural diversity. By documenting these communities' customs, landscapes, and artistic expressions, he expresses their present realities and plays a crucial part in promoting their recognition and conservation.

His documentaries make a substantial contribution to cultural studies and visual anthropology. They are vital resources for scholarly research and public debate that enable a critical analysis of topics like regional identity, cultural heritage, and ecological sustainability.

He made 31 documentaries and received nine National Awards for his documentaries, which include: *Sangai: The Dancing Deer of Manipur* (1988), *Deer on the Lake* (1989), *Indigenous Games of Manipur* (1990), *Meitei Pung* (1991), *Orchids of Manipur* (1993), *Yelhou Jagoi* (1995), *Thang-Ta: Martial Arts of Manipur* (1999), *The Monpas of Arunachal Pradesh* (2001), *Guru Laimayum Thambalngoubi* (2006), and *Manipuri Pony* (2012).

Pabung's *Tales of Courage* (1986), produced by the Films Division of India, is a notable Manipuri documentary. In the larger framework of India's independence movement, this documentary pays homage to Manipur's outstanding contributions. The film traces back the rich history of Manipur and its role in the fight against British colonial rule. It begins its narrative in 1857, when Manipur was under the rule of Maharaja Chandra Kirti Singh. This period marked the emergence of significant resistance against British authority, and the documentary shows the bravery and determination of the Manipuri people during this tumultuous time.

A key figure in the documentary is Manipuri prince Narendrajit Singh, who emerged as a leader among the revolutionaries serving in the 34th Native Infantry. His courageous actions against British forces represented the spirit of resistance. Sadly, his bravery led to his capture, and he was subsequently exiled to the Andaman Islands, a place known for its harsh penal settlement. Despite such severe repercussions, his actions inspired many others in Manipur and beyond to join the fight for freedom.

Throughout the documentary, we are introduced to various freedom fighters from Manipur who displayed extraordinary valour and strength. By chronicling these events and individuals, *Tales of Courage* not only preserves the legacy of Manipur's role in India's freedom struggle but also instils a sense of pride among us. Through a blend of historical narratives, personal accounts, and evocative visuals, the film reflects on the sacrifices made for freedom.

His documentary *Koro Kosii* (The gate, 1988) is about the celebration of the erection of the village gate by the Mao tribe in Manipur. In the heart of a Mao Naga village, the remarkable ritual known as "Koro Kosii," or the gate-pulling ceremony, unfolds—a ceremonial event deeply deep-rooted in cultural heritage, occurring only once every forty to fifty years. Situated within the majestic northern ranges of Manipur, the Mao Nagas represent an ancient lineage of formidable warriors. Within this societal structure, each village is governed by a chief; however, all subjects pledge their loyalty to a singular, revered figure—the Muovo—who represents the unity and cohesion among the various clans. The essence of these villages is vividly captured in their imposing fortifications, which are constructed from pointed bamboo stakes that rise ominously like vigilant sentinels. At either entrance to this formidable enclosure stand the Koros— two intricately carved wooden gates, each hewn from a single, monumental plank. These gates transcend their functional role as mere barriers; they work as potent symbols of both temporal and divine protection. It signifies the lasting bond between the villagers and their ancestral spirits. Within the confines of the village, the memory of the last Koro Kosii ceremony has long since dissipated into the annals of communal consciousness. However, during the momentous occasion depicted in the film, the ceremony catalysed a transformation of the mundane into the extraordinary over the course of two exhilarating days. Through heartfelt chants and collaborative efforts, the villagers harnessed their collective strength and solidarity, renewing the sacred bond that links them to their land and traditions. Thus, the mighty gates ascended once more, standing resolutely as sentinels—vigilant guardians of the village, prepared to oversee the generations yet to come.

Koro Kosii transcended the conventional boundaries of cinematic storytelling; it emerged as a profound portal into the essence of the Mao Naga people. Through its narrative, Koro Kosii draws the enduring spirit of a community that, despite the passage of time, remains intricately tied to its ancestral roots and cultural identity. The documentary received recognition at prestigious film festivals such as the Indian Film Week in Hungary, the Mumbai International Film Festival in 1988, and the International Film Festival of India (IFFI) in 1989.

Sangai: Resonating broader themes of cultural preservation

Pabung's seminal documentary *Sangai: The Dancing Deer of Manipur*, produced by the Sangeet Natak Akademi in 1988, is an essential cultural work that capture the intricate interconnection between nature, culture, and performance art in Manipur. The 46-minute film received significant acclaim, including recognition from the British Film Institute as the Outstanding Film of the Year in 1989. More than a mere portrayal of dance, *Sangai* is a powerful visual narrative that threads together the ecological plight of a species—the Sangai (the dancing deer), with the cultural and artistic expressions of the Manipuri people. This documentary not only expresses the unique biotic diversity of the region but also gives essential observation on the socio-ecological dynamics inherent to Manipuri identity. At its core, *Sangai* draws upon the intricate dance-drama "Keibul Lamjao," choreographed by Chaaotombi Singh and performed by the Jawaharlal Nehru Manipur Dance Academy. This work demonstrates how contemporary Indian choreography can reflect environmental awareness. It powerfully conveys messages about conservation and cultural identity through performance.

The documentary, *Sangai* begins by establishing a connection between the physical environment and the cultural practices of the Manipuri people. The Sangai, or dancing deer, is a symbol of the region's ecological richness and reminds us of the threats posed to this biodiversity. The deer's graceful movements, characterized by elegance and fluidity, are paralleled in the traditional dances. The Keibul Lamjao National Park, depicted in the documentary, represents more than just a habitat for the Sangai; it becomes a space where cultural rituals and artistic expressions converge. This unique location, famous for being the world's only floating national park, represents how natural landscapes shape cultural identities. The documentary shows how the Manipuri people's artistic expressions intricately reflect their strong ties to the land and its creatures. This representation promotes more environmental awareness and a feeling of cultural preservation.

The significance of the Sangai extends beyond its biological classification; it represents the intertwined destinies of species and human communities. Historically, the Sangai has faced challenges, including habitat loss and poaching, that prompted urgent conversations about wildlife conservation and cultural identity. The documentary illustrates that the plight of the Sangai is representative of a larger narrative concerning human impacts on ecology. The Sangai is a regional race of the brow-antlered deer, now confined to a small population within Keibul Lamjao National Park. With numbers dwindling to as few as one hundred individuals, the Sangai's situation points out the broader implications of biodiversity loss. The film uses the narrative of the Sangai's plight as a vehicle to address essential questions about conservation and sustainability. As the audience learns about the deer's existence and fragility, they are invited to consider their own roles in preserving such ecosystems and cultural legacies.

Central to the documentary is the dance-drama "Keibul Lamjao." The performance is an artistic retelling of a Manipuri legend that carries deep emotional and cultural resonance. The protagonist, Kadeng, represents the human ambition to conquer nature but also reflects the inevitable consequences of such endeavors. Leading a hunting expedition ordered by the king, Kadeng, captures a Sangai to fulfil a wish for his betrothed, Tonu, yet returns only to find her lost to the king's whims. This poignant narrative has dual purpose: as a vehicle for storytelling and as a means of critiquing the ecological abuses stemming from human desires. The choreography attracts not only the beauty of the Sangai but also its struggle against forces beyond its control. The movements of the dancers are inspired by the delicate grace of the deer, forming an evocative link that reinforces the intertwined themes of nature and performance art. The film draws the dynamism of this dance, employing cinematic techniques that amplify its physicality, rhythm, and expression.

The documentary features a combination of close-up shots, wide angles, and slow-motion sequences that create a rich visual element. The use of traditional Manipuri music complements the visual fundamentals. This synergy between sound and movement elevates the storytelling. By harnessing the language of film to present traditional dance, Pabung demonstrates how modern mediums can be used to conserve and convey cultural heritage.

Though Sangai is rooted firmly in traditional cultural contexts, it opens up broader discussions about contemporary challenges facing indigenous peoples and their ecosystems. The film's narrative structure reflects a conscious effort to elevate the plight of the Sangai as emblematic of the struggles faced by various species worldwide in the face of human encroachment. By embedding the story of the Sangai within the medium of dance, Pabung also sets the relationship between ecological preservation and cultural identity. Through the narrative of Kadeng, Pabung Aribam presents a multifaceted view of human intervention in nature—one that is both transformative and destructive. The abduction of Tonu, coupled with Kadeng's betrayal of the Sangai for personal gain, serves as a larger commentary on the exploitation of natural resources for human satisfaction. This narrative amplifies important questions around conservation: What are the ethical obligations of humans in relation to other species? How can cultural narratives help shape an ethos of ecological sustainability?

By employing the dance-drama format, *Sangai* advocates for an ethical stewardship towards the environment. While deeply rooted in the socio-cultural fabric of Manipur, Sangai echoes broader themes of cultural preservation in an increasingly globalized world. As traditional practices confront the challenges of modernisation and cultural homogenisation, the documentary shows the spirit of local identities. Pabung's work stands as an example of how indigenous narratives must be cherished and propagated, particularly in a context where environmental degradation threatens both the land and its people.

Sangai is a critical counter-narrative to the dominant discourses surrounding wildlife conservation, which can often marginalize indigenous perspectives. By elevating the local narrative, Pabung Aribam positions the themes of ecological preservation firmly within the cultural context of Manipur. His *Sangai: The Dancing Deer of Manipur* represents a reflective cultural exploration that interweaves nature, identity, and ecological preservation.

His documentary *The Deer on the Lake* (1989) powerfully explains the critical situation facing the brow-antlered deer, commonly known as Sangai. This elegant and unique species, which is native to the wetlands of Manipur in India, is teetering on the edge of extinction, with a population that has dwindled to approximately fifty individuals. The documentary is as both a touching narrative and an urgent call to action, that explores several reasons behind the Sangai's endangered status. One of the central themes of the documentary is the exploration of the environmental changes affecting Keibul Lamjao, the sole habitat of the Sangai. It shows how factors such as habitat degradation, climate change, and human encroachment are disrupting the delicate ecosystem that supports these deer. With rising water levels and shifting vegetation patterns, the natural balance that has sustained the Sangai for centuries is gradually threatened. The documentary aims to raise awareness about these pressing environmental issues and their direct impact on the survival of this remarkable species.

In addition to its gripping narrative, *The Deer on the Lake* has been recognized for its significant contributions to environmental conservation. It was honored with the National Award for Best Environmental Conservation and Preservation Film in 1990. It r also won a Merit Award for its portrayal of endangered species at the 12th Annual International Wildlife Film Festival in Montana, USA, in 1989.

The documentary, *The Meitei Pung* (1991), is about the use of the double-headed drum, called Pung, in the religious and cultural life of the Meitei community. This documentary gives us a deep and insightful exploration of the Meitei Pung, a barrel-shaped drum. It is not just a musical instrument but a vital thread woven into the fabric of Manipuri culture. This documentary portrays how the Meitei Pung is a powerful medium of expression and connection for the Manipuri people. At the heart of the documentary is the drum's significance in various musical celebrations, particularly those honouring Lord

Krishna. These celebrations are vibrant and lively. They are often characterized by intricate dance forms and communal participation. The sound of the Meitei Pung becomes a rhythmic beat that unites the performers and the audience alike. The drum's beats create an atmosphere of joy and spirituality. Dancers depend on the drum's rhythm to express their movements, expressing the stories and emotions conveyed through the dance. The documentary draws the interaction between the musicians and dancers, that illustrates how the drum's intricate taals—rhythmic patterns—bring depth and dynamism to the performances. Made from local materials—wood and leather—the Meitei Pung is not only a product of artistic skill but also a representation of the region's natural resources and craftsmanship. *The Meitei Pung* is not just a documentary about a musical instrument; it is a celebration of a rich cultural heritage that continues to thrive through music, dance, and community.

In recognition of its artistic and cultural importance, the documentary *The Meitei Pung* was awarded a Special Jury Mention at the National Awards in 1992 and also it was screened at the International Film Festival of India (IFFI).

Pabung Aribam, a filmmaker with profound cultural roots, has undertaken extensive documentation on the Dhummel, a unique form of Sankirtana centred around the Pung (traditional drum). In a recent personal communication, Pabung

Aribam shared insights from his comprehensive research, saying that Dhummel is a distinct and significant branch of Manipuri Nata-Sankirtana. According to Pabung Aribam, Dhummel itself is a specialised form of Sankirtana with four recognised types: Maha Dhummel; Goura Dhummel; Nityai Dhummel and Devi or Lairembi Dhummel. Maha Dhummel is a classical variant of Sankirtana introduced by King Bhagyachandra, who was also instrumental in developing the renowned Manipuri Raas tradition. This elaborate performance features fourteen percussionists or drummers, making a grand and intricate musical arrangement. The Maha Dhummel is deeply linked with Vaishnava philosophy, particularly the concept of "Astakaal", which describes the eight periods of the day, each associated with a specific episode from the stories of Radha and Krishna. Goura Dhummel was composed during the reign of King Gambhir Singh, adding another distinct dimension to the repertoire of Nata-Sankirtana. Nityai Dhummel is traditionally performed at the conclusion of Sankirtana ceremonies. Historical records note its presentation by King Chaurajit at the Langthabal palace, marking it as an integral part of the ceremonial closing. Lastly, Devi or Lairembi Dhummel is performed exclusively during Durga Puja, that shows its significance within the context of ritual worship and celebration. Through his meticulous documentation, Pabung Aribam has illuminated the rich diversity and cultural depth of the Dhummel tradition, that focuses on its role within the broader landscape of Manipuri performing arts.

Pabung Aribam's documentary *Lai Haraoba* (1992), produced by the Indira Gandhi National Centre for the Arts in New Delhi, was conceptualized by Dr. Kapila Vatsyayan and directed by Aribam Syam Sharma. This film intricately explores the Lai Haraoba, an annual ritual festival celebrated by the people of the Manipur valley, embodying the myth of the universe's creation, encompassing heaven, earth, and light as they manifest in flora, fauna, humanity, and the evolution of civilization. Traditionally held from April to May, Lai Haraoba can last for 7, 9, 13 days, or even longer. It is performed in four recognized variations: Chakpa Haraoba, Kanglei Haraoba, Moirang Haraoba, and Kakching Haraoba, typically taking place in courtyards or open spaces of local shrines dedicated to the Umang Lai deities. The entire community engages in the Lai Haraoba ceremony, aimed at pleasing the deities, with the belief that it brings prosperity, happiness, and self-realization. The rituals are conducted by the maibas, maibis, and penakhongbas, each with distinct roles. The maibas adhere to the "Loisang," a religious code of ministration, ensuring that every detail of the sacred ceremony is executed flawlessly. While the maibis have specific ritual responsibilities, it is the maibis who hold the exclusive privilege of lighting the ceremonial fires, caring for them, and performing songs and dances. A day before the festival, or on the day itself, two icons are crafted from bamboo cane, resembling human forms adorned with elaborate decorations, along with images featuring brass-plated faces.

Filmmaker Pabung goes deep in detailing each and everything of the festival in the 70 minutes long duration documentary. In the documentary, Pabung uses ritual dances, dramatic performances, and grand processions as its narrative devices, which suggests that these elements are intrinsic to the spiritual and communal identity of Manipuri society.

Pabung begins the documentary with with the Meitei Manuscript text on creation of universe. It states, "Atingkok Sidaba asks Atiya Sidaba to create the world. Atiya is perplexed and asks his Father, 'How and what should I create?' Atingkok opens His mouth and reveals everything within Him. The sun, the moon, the stars, galaxies, fire, water, air, and all other phenomena are in Him. In reverential awe, Atiya asks Him to close His mouth. However, with an urge to draw all those phenomena out into the open, Atiya enters Atingkok. He tries to drive the phenomena out by singing the divine song 'Hoirou.' As they resist him, Atingkok creates another self outside Himself. The phenomena within Him, deluded by the vision of the other self, rush out. Atingkok opens His mouth and receives those driven out by Atiya with the divine song 'Haya.' The song of those coming out resounds through the sacred song 'Ha Hoi Hoi,' an expression of their happiness."

Regarding the phenomena of *Lai Haraoba,* Dr. Nganbi Chanu writes in her article "Ritual Festival for

Appeasing Ancestral Gods: A Study of Kanglei Lai-haraoba Festival of Manipur," published in the *Journal of North East India Studies* (Vol. 4(1), Jan.-Jul. 2014, pp. 43-54.). Dr. Chanu focuses on the challenges faced in preserving the texts of the Lai-Haraoba festival. She notes that many texts were lost due to wars and religious persecution, resulting in a reliance on secondary sources composed of fragments from surviving puyas in the form of manuscripts. The preservation of this rich oral tradition has primarily been attributed to three key figures: the Amaiba (Priest), the Amaibi (Priestess), and the Penakhongba/Pena Asheiba (Pena player/singer), who have diligently passed down these traditions through generations.

Dr. Chanu elaborates that *Lai-Haraoba* is a significant ritual festival in Manipur, celebrated for centuries to honour ancestral deities. The festival enacts the creation of the universe and its essence, seeking blessings from these deities in return. It illustrates the origins of life emerging from the cosmic creation, emphasizing the union of the Supreme Male (pa principle) and Supreme Female (pi principle), symbolized by Father Sky and Mother Earth, through daily rituals. The festival features symbolic performances and objects that represent the process of creation, including the act of sexual intercourse. The daily rituals starting from the first day to the last day of the festival comprise of the development of universe, the growth of human beings and society, having images right from the beginning. It can be said that the chief and internal motivation of this so called festival "Lai-Haraoba" is procreation vitality, abundance and healthy community life.

Sohini Ray, a former fellow at the University of California Humanities Research Institute in Irvine, offers an engaging exploration of *Lai Haraoba* in her article titled "Writing the Body: Cosmology, Orthography, and Fragments of Modernity in Northeastern India," published in *Anthropological Quarterly*. Under the subheading "Cosmology of Gestures," Ray investigates the philosophical dimensions of *Lai Haraoba*, illuminating a vital aspect of Meitei culture that centers around the body. She interprets the Meitei script as an extension of the body itself, providing insightful context for the diverse spectrum of performing arts in Manipur. This perspective not only enhances our understanding of the cultural significance of gestures but also explains the deep connections between body, language, and artistic expression within the Meitei tradition.

In her article, she writes, "During this festival, the women priestesses, known as maibis, propitiate the indigenous deity by performing a variety of intricate dances. One of the dances that is obligatorily performed in front of the god is the profound enactment of the creation of the body."

Ray quotes T. Maibi, who expresses that the navel aperture in the human body holds significance akin to that of a sacred pilgrimage site; it is atop this spot that a lotus blooms, symbolizing the presence of the guru or Supreme Being, whose shadow gracefully falls upon the water. The narrative describes Atiya guru sidaba, the Supreme Being, who once existed as a bird, transformed into a toad, and after undergoing a series of incarnations, ultimately led to the creation of the human body by observing the guru's shadow. Within the body of a pregnant woman, the child exists in the nurturing waters, growing daily from the navel. As the child develops over the course of 364 days, the initial stage lasts for 64 days, followed by a later stage of 300 days. The 64 hand gestures employed in the dance that depict the formation of the human body represent these 64 days, and subsequently, 300 gestures are added, resulting in a total of 364 gestures.

Ray examines the dance performed during *Lai Haraoba*, exploring its intricate relationship with the philosophy of the body. She cites T. Maibi, who posits that the dance serves as a celebration of nature's process of life replication, thereby honouring the very process through which life is created. The act of dancing signifies the making of the first body in the universe, the body of the Supreme Being. The visualization of the human body, along with the attempt to correlate the number of gestures with the birth cycle, provides yet another compelling illustration of the pervasive cosmological principles inherent in the Meitei faith. The *Lai Haraoba* festival itself symbolizes the very act of universal creation, and the ritual performances of body-making dances during the festival underscore the formation of the Supreme Being's body, the same body from which the letters of the 27-letter alphabet are derived. This ritual performance of body-making is meticulously accomplished through a series of hand gestures. The 64 hand gestures and their connection to the days in the gestation cycle of a human infant unveil a profound cosmic pattern. Ray states, 'even though the cosmology of the body described here differs considerably from that described earlier in this essay, this variation of the body cosmology is yet another example of the cultural schema of the body in the Meitei society.'

Pabung's documentary *Lai Haraoba* (1992) is a visually rich and aesthetically captivating work, meticulously researched and extremely treasured for both academic and cultural study. This documentary is undeniably a masterpiece.

Another significant documentary by Pabung Aribam is *Orchids of Manipur* (1993). This film shows the unique varieties of Manipuri orchids and explores their connection to local legends, daily life, and the broader cultural heritage of Manipur. It begins with a folk song narrating the birth of a flower. As the song unfolds, from the northern heights of the sacred Koubiu Mountains, Lord Pakhangba descends into the valley with Goddess Laishana. Along the way, when the path bifurcates, the king of gods settles, leaving his daughter Ponjenbi and her mother Laishana behind. The Lord ascends the hill of Nangmaiching to plant trees. Meanwhile, Goddess Laishana lies on her deathbed, and her daughter's grief-stricken wails fill the heavens. Hearing the cry, Pakhangba rushes down, only to find his beloved has passed away. With a heavy heart, he buries her and places a huge slab of rock on her grave. The following year, he discovers a flower in full bloom on the grave. The flower enchants the heart of the mighty warrior king, who believes it to be an expression of Laishana's love. He names it Meitei Laishang Nongjumpal, meaning "the flower of love in the wilderness." This is how the story unfolds.

In the voice-over, it is noted that much of Manipur consists of mountainous territory. In the thick forests, colorful orchids grow on gigantic trees. Manipur is truly a garden of orchids, with climatic conditions perfectly suited for their growth. In the documentary, the flowers are shown dancing with the rhythm of the Manipuri music. 'According to the movement and rhythm of the flowers, the music is incorporated in the documentary', says Pabung to this author.

Produced by the Indira Gandhi National Centre for the Arts, New Delhi, *Yelhou Jagoi* (1995) is a powerful visual ethnography that clearly shows the rich culture of the Manipur valley through its yearly festival. The documentary focuses on a re-enactment of the creation myth, reflecting local beliefs about the universe. The creation myth portrays the link between the sky, the land, and all living things (plants, animals, and people). One of the documentary's important points is the depiction of the Maibies' dance, a potent cultural expression through which the growth of a child is symbolically represented. The choreography is meticulously constructed to embody the stages of development—from the embryonic phase within the womb to the complexities of adulthood. Notably, it uses a lexicon of 364 distinct hand movements that serve as both a narrative mechanism and a performative language. Each movement and gesture is immersed in cultural significance, that displays various rites of passage and human activities such as housing construction, agriculture, and fishing.

The documentary does not merely document the festival; but focuses on the rituals that shape communal identity and continuity. By comparing personal achievements with collective celebrations, it shows how individual growth connects to society as a whole. Premised on anthropological inquiry, *Yelhou Jagoi* is a fundamental record of the socio-cultural dynamics of Manipur. It offers a thoughtful way to understand how ritual, identity, and the environment are connected. The documentary was selected as the opening film of the Indian Panorama at the 1996 International Film Festival of India and won National Award for Best Anthropological and Ethnographical Film.

Pabung Aribam's documentary *Thang-Ta: Martial Art of Manipur* (1999), presented by the Indira Gandhi National Centre for the Arts, explores the Manipuri martial art known as Thang-Ta (sword and spear), which is dedicated to both combat skills and worship. It begins with the myth of Atingkok Shidaba, the eternal one, who commanded his son Ashiba to create the universe. Ashiba found the task too overwhelming to accomplish alone and, from his essence, manifested nine male deities known as Laibungthous. These deities participated in an esoteric exercise called Thengou during the creation process. Four of the Laibungthous executed a sequence of three steps known as "Leihou Thengou," thus forming the Earth, while the other four performed "Nonghou Thengou," which consists of five steps, shaping the sky. According to the Meitei creation myth, the movements involved in this creation process, ritualized as "Thengou," are believed to represent the original movement patterns foundational to Thang-Ta, the martial art of Manipur.

The voiceover narrates how, over the ages, the Manipuris developed a distinct martial art form known as Thang-Ta. Throughout history, the people of this small kingdom were able to defeat the armies of Burma and neighbouring countries through the culture surrounding this art. A notable exponent of Thang-Ta is Paona Brajabasi, who sacrificed his life during the Anglo-Manipuri War of 1891 and is still remembered with reverence by the people of Manipur. Following that battle in 1891, the kingdom was annexed by the British, leading to a ban on the practice of this art form, with the possession of swords and spears punishable by death or exile. Nevertheless, Thang-Ta endured through the secret schools maintained by masters and apprentices.

The documentary traces the profound connections between the martial and spiritual aspects of Thang-Ta. It shows how these elements are deeply woven into the psyche of the Manipuri people. It demonstrates how the rigorous physicality of this martial art is not merely about combat and self-defence but also serves as a form of spiritual expression and cultural identity. Through visual storytelling and interviews, the documentary elucidates how practitioners engage in not only the technical execution of movements but also in rituals that honour their traditions and deities. The documentary affirms Thang-Ta's lasting significance as a living tradition that preserves and strengthens the cultural heritage of the Manipuri community in the face of modern challenges.

The Marams (1999) produced by Directorate of Tribals and Backward Classes, Govt. of Manipur, presents an appealing exploration of the monolithic tradition within the Maram community, an indigenous tribe located in the vibrant North-Eastern state of Manipur, India. This unique practice stands out even among the rich mosaic of ethnic groups that populate the region, each with its own customs and cultural heritage. What is particularly interesting about the Marams' monoliths are their remarkable construction and placement. Unlike many other cultural practices where monuments are often embedded or supported by the earth, these monoliths are strikingly positioned upright on the surface, seemingly defying the laws of physics. They stand tall and proud, without any visible means of support, making their presence all the more intriguing. The process behind creating and erecting these monoliths speaks volumes about the technical skills and spiritual beliefs of the Maram community. These monoliths are not merely physical structures; they hold deep significance in the community. They often mark important events or honouring ancestors, that works as a bridge between the past and the present.

Pabung Aribam's documentary, *The Monpas of Arunachal Pradesh* (2001), produced by Films Division, scripted by Pabung's son, Aribam Gautam, unfolds as a visual poem, rich in imagery and lyrical in its narration. Through evocative cinematography, the film paints a vivid portrait of the distinctive lifestyle, customs, rituals, and traditions of the Monpa tribe, an indigenous tribe residing in the North-Eastern state of Arunachal Pradesh.

The opening sequence lingers on a herd of yaks as a Monpa herder gently feeds them straw. The serene visuals are accompanied by the soft cadence of a traditional song, immersing us in the rhythm of Monpa life. This ethnographic documentary reflects Pabung Aribam's deep conviction and respect for his subject. One memorable scene features a local Monpa explaining, "We are the caretakers of the yaks. We stay at this altitude because yaks prefer it. They cannot survive in the lowlands. Yaks are very precious to the people here; they are an important means of transport in this difficult terrain. Besides being beasts of burden, they provide us with many things—from their hair, we make clothes and shoes; they also give us milk. We use the milk to make ghee and cheese. The first ghee we make is offered at the Gompa as a lamp offering to Lord Buddha, a practice rooted in our faith."

As the documentary progresses, it shifts its focus to Tawang—the westernmost district of Arunachal Pradesh, bordering Bhutan and Tibet, and home to the Monpas, the largest Buddhist tribe in the state. The narrative focuses on Tawang Gompa, the heart of Monpa spiritual and cultural life, majestically perched at 10,000 feet above sea level. Its full name, Galden Namgyal Lhatse, means "the celestial paradise". The monastery houses a 36-foot statue of Lord Buddha in the main prayer hall, known as the *Dokhang*, that stands as a centrepiece of devotion. The Gompa, founded by Mera Lama with the blessings of the Fifth Dalai Lama, is a beacon of the Gelugpa sect of Mahayana Buddhism and is considered the second oldest monastery in the world. The film also introduces us to Urgelling Gompa, located three kilometres from Tawang, revered as the birthplace of the Sixth Dalai Lama, Tsangyang Tashi.

The Monpas practice the Lamaist Mahayana school of Buddhism. Both monks and village priests are known as Lamas, and tradition dictates that in families with three sons, the second son must be sent to the monastery. The documentary offers a poignant example through the story of Loksondawa, who, though he has only two sons, sends his younger boy,

Pasang, to the Gompa, earning admiration and respect in his community. The age for joining the monastery is flexible, typically between five and twelve years old, reflecting the community's deep-rooted spiritual values.

The Monpas are portrayed as resourceful and self-reliant people, guided by a simple, meaningful code of life inspired by their faith. Agriculture forms the backbone of their economy, with both shifting and permanent cultivation practices, along with a keen understanding of soil enrichment. Monpa women, artistic by nature, weave their garments on simple, portable looms and craft vibrant carpets adorned with exquisite dragon motifs.

Life's milestones are marked by heartfelt rituals. The birth of a child is celebrated with joy; within a week, both mother and child are given a ceremonial bath, and a village Lama is invited to perform purification rituals, cast the horoscope, and bestow a name. Well-wishers gather to offer "chang", a local brew, wishing prosperity to the newborn and family.

The documentary also focuses on the Torgya festival, the grand monastic dance performances. People perform the Lamaistic dances to ward off evil spirits and promote communal well-being.

Pabung shared with me that his fascination with Buddhism began during his time pursuing a master's degree in philosophy at Santiniketan. Reflecting on those formative years, he recalls, "My interest in Buddhism truly took root during my days at Santiniketan. It was there that I learnt about Buddhism's arrival in Manipur and its subsequent struggle to establish a lasting presence. This realisation prompted me to explore the reasons behind Buddhism's inability to take root in Manipur." His quest for understanding led him to study the Monpa community of Arunachal Pradesh and to visit the rich Buddhist traditions preserved within the last surviving monasteries of Northeast India. Immersing himself in Buddhist philosophy had a profound influence on him, especially the timeless invocation "Buddham saranam gacchami, Dhammam saranam gacchami"—meaning "I go to the Buddha for refuge; I go to the Dhamma for refuge." Inspired by these teachings and the spiritual journeys they represent, Pabung chose to name his son Gautam in honour of the Buddha.

I would like to mention another aspect of Pabung that is reflected in his films, including this documentary. Pabung uses Japanese culture as a way to better understand Meitei culture, especially its syncretic traits. This shows how Meitei culture is a mix of different influences, especially those from the *Lai-Haraoba* and Vaishnavism, which has had a big effect on the area. Syncretism is an important part of how cultures change over time. It is the mixing of different religious, cultural, and philosophical traditions. As cultural studies say, "syncretism is not just a mix of two different things; it is a complex interaction that makes a new identity." In the case of Meitei culture, this phenomenon is evident in how indigenous practices, such as those celebrated during the *Lai-Haraoba*, have integrated with the doctrines and rituals of Vaishnavism, a prominent form of Hinduism that focuses on devotion to Lord Vishnu. This has made a unique cultural landscape where traditional Meitei beliefs mix with religious ideas from outside the community. *Lai-Haraoba* is an important part of Meitei culture. It includes ritual dances, music, and stories that honour the creation myths and gods of the Manipuri pantheon. This festival shows off the Meitei people's rich culture and spirituality, as well as their community life. However, the arrival of Vaishnavism added new layers of religious and artistic meaning to this cultural expression. Pabung shows how both the Meitei and Japanese cultures are very good at mixing different cultural elements while still keeping their own unique identities. Japanese culture combines Shinto beliefs with Buddhist practices, creating a rich and harmonious cultural landscape. Similarly, Meitei culture is a mix of its original traditions and those brought in by Vaishnavism. This mixing of cultures makes the Meitei experience richer, with a wide range of artistic expressions, idioms, and practices that show how the community's history and ability to adapt to new influences have shaped it. The way these different cultural strands interact with each other not only makes Meitei expressions more unique, but it also shows how cultures change over time. Pabung Aribam says that "the essence of culture lies in its ability to evolve and adapt, drawing from a variety of sources to create something uniquely its own."

For me, *The Monpas of Arunachal Pradesh* transcends the boundaries of a mere documentary—it stands as a cinematic poem, elegantly showing the spirit, and beauty of the Monpa people along with their enduring traditions. In recognition of its excellence and contribution to ethnographic cinema, the film was featured in the Indian Panorama section of the International Film Festival of India (IFFI) in 2001. It garnered critical acclaim, winning two prestigious National Awards: one for Best Anthropological and Ethnographical Film and another for Best Cinematographer (This award was for the cameraman, Irom Maipak).

The documentary *Rajarshi Bhagyachandra* (2006), produced by Films Division and showcased at the Indian Panorama in 2007, shifts the focus to the historical and cultural figure of Bhagyachandra, who is heralded as the greatest Vaishnavite king of Manipur. The film explores his dual identity as both a valiant strategist and a protector of his land and people, wielding his sword in defense of their sovereignty. However, beyond his martial prowess, Bhagyachandra is also celebrated as a creative luminary who significantly advanced the classical dance form known as Manipuri raas. This duality of his character shows the multifaceted nature of leadership where strength and artistry coalesce. It illustrates how Bhagyachandra's legacy is not only one of military might but also of cultural enrichment and artistic innovation within the Manipuri cultural milieu.

His two documentaries *Manipuri Pony* (2012) and *The Indigenous Games of Manipur* (1990) deal with the small horse or pony used in the polo games, and the polo game, which is traditionally known as Sagol Kangei. The documentary, *Manipuri Pony*, speaks of the significance of Sagol Kangjei, the traditional Manipuri game that is the precursor to modern polo, which extends beyond its historical and cultural roots; it embodies complex intersections of identity, heritage, and the contemporary challenges faced by the Manipuri Pony, the animal central to this cultural practice. Initially introduced to the British in the mid-nineteenth century, Sagol Kangjei not only popularized the game internationally but also highlighted the rich cultural landscape of Manipur. The propagation of this sport initiated a global appreciation for Manipuri culture, yet it also set in motion a series of historical shifts that would ultimately threaten the very essence of that culture—the Manipuri Pony.

L. Somi Roy, a cultural conservationist and social thinker from Manipur, states in an interview featured in the documentary that between 1844 and 1850, while the infant king, Chandrakirti was in exile with his mother in Cachar, Assam, soldiers in exile were observed playing a game they called "hockey on horseback." The establishment of the Silchar Polo Club in 1859, recognized as the world's first polo club, was influenced by the Meitei soldiers whom traders from the East India Company, particularly those involved in the tea trade, which had begun around 10 to 15 years earlier in Assam, saw playing polo. During this period, British soldiers and traders began learning hockey on horseback from the Meitei soldiers. A British Army officer and survivor of the Sepoy Mutiny, traveled to Manipur and brought a team of Meitei polo players with him. In 1863, the first Manipuri *sagol kangjei* (horse hockey) exhibition was held in Calcutta at the Baliganj Cricket Club. From that moment, it captivated all of British India and eventually reached Queen Victoria, leading to its introduction in London, where the first game of polo was played at the Hurlingham Club, becoming the main sport there in 1869. Therefore, from 1844 to 1869, polo began to establish itself, and the rules began to evolve.

In the documentary, the filmmaker informs us about the origins of polo using slides from the Guinness Book of Records (1991), which authenticated the game's origin. Polo can be traced to its roots in Manipur State around 3100 B.C., where it was played as *Sagol Kangjei* Other claims suggest that it has Persian origins, having been played as pulu around 525 B.C. The game was introduced to British officers in Cachar by the Manipur Maharaja Shri Chandrakirti Singh, and the earliest club was the Cachar Club, founded in 1859 in Assam, India. The oldest club still in existence is the Calcutta Polo Club, which was established in 1862. The game was introduced to England from India in 1869 by the 10th Hussars at Aldershot, Hants.

The evolution of Sagol Kangjei into polo reflects broader themes of colonialism and cultural exchange. While the game gained international acclaim, the commodification of the sport often overlooked the underlying significance of the Manipuri Pony, an animal deeply intertwined with the cultural identity of the Manipuri people. The pony, known for its agility and endurance, became emblematic of the region's heritage. Despite its precarious status, the continuing efforts to conserve the Manipuri Pony signify a resilient cultural identity that refuses to fade into obscurity. The hope for the survival of the Manipuri Pony is not merely about saving an endangered species; it is a struggle to maintain a vital link to the historical and cultural narrative of Manipur.

The recognition of the documentary *Manipuri Pony* through various film festivals and awards serves as a crucial platform for raising awareness about this issue. The film's awards, including the National Award for Best Exploration/Adventure Film and screenings at prestigious festivals, illustrate the power of visual storytelling in fostering cultural advocacy.

The documentary, *The Indigenous Games of Manipur* explores the rich cultural heritage of Manipur through its traditional sports. The film highlights several indigenous games, each reflecting the unique traditions and values of the Manipuri people. Games like *Cheibi* (a traditional wrestling sport), *Mukna* (a form of wrestling with unique techniques), *Yubi lakpi* (a traditional game similar to rugby), *Mukna Kangjei* (a blend of martial arts and hockey), *Hiyang* (a form of boat racing), *Kang* (a traditional game involving skill and strategy), and *Sagol kangjei* (Manipuri polo) are showcased, illustrating their historical significance and the role they play in community bonding and cultural identity. Through vivid imagery and storytelling, the documentary not only preserves these games but also emphasizes their importance in maintaining the cultural fabric of Manipur amidst modernization.

Pabung's documentaries are a vital medium for examining the complexities of identity, tradition, and modernity in Indian society, particularly in the North-East. By spotlighting lesser-known communities and their practices, he offers invaluable insights into the region's rich cultural landscape, which is often underrepresented in mainstream narratives. This emphasis not only reflects the importance of cultural preservation but also challenges dominant discourses that frequently neglect the nuances of indigenous identities.

According to Kongbam (2020), Aribam "made all his documentaries by significantly identifying and highlighting the important aspects of a subject, tracing it from its origin and coming down to the contemporary situation." Aribam's documentaries are as significant as his fictional feature films. They function not only as artistic endeavors but also as essential contributions to the discourse on identity, tradition, and the preservation of cultural heritage in an increasingly globalized world. The recognition Aribam has received, including nine National Awards for his documentaries and the Dr. V. Shantaram Lifetime Achievement Award, highlights the critical acclaim of his work within the broader discourse of documentary cinema.

***

Works Cited

Kongbam, M. (2020). Aribam Syam Sharma: A Genius of Indian cinema. In *Article* (p. 1). http://www.fipresci-india.org/wp-content/uploads/2020/04/05.-Meghachandra-Kongbam-Aribam-Syam-Sharma-A-Genius-of-Indian-Cinema.pdf

Ray, S. *Anthropological Quarterly*, Vol. 82, No. 1, pp. 129–154, ISSN 0003-549. © 2009 by the Institute for Ethnographic Research (IFER) a part of the George Washington University.

Sharma, A. S. (2006). *Living shadows*. Gauhati Cine Club. Guwahati, Assam.

Chapter Six

Narrative Aesthetics: The Beauty of Visual Storytelling

Pabung Aribam's cinematic approach is steeped in poetic elegance, marked by lyrical aesthetics and the art of visual storytelling. His cinematic vision is intricately woven into the rich cultural fabric of Manipur, engaging a rhythmical narrative technique that profoundly connects with audiences. From his debut film, *Lamja Parshuram*, to his latest work, *Nongphadok Lakpa Atithi*, his method remains lucid and unembellished. He avoids elaborate subplots and complex character arcs, opting instead for a contemplative viewing experience that invites reflection. This focus on transparency and lyricism transcends mere stylistic choice; it creates an environment where audience can engage with the narrative easily. His films illustrate a mastery of craft, characterised by striking visuals and profound emotional and cultural relevance that endures beyond the final minutes of the film.

The purity of his narrative reflects his unwavering commitment to authenticity. He crafts stories that remain true to their cultural contexts, often rooted in the rich heritage of his native Manipur. The authenticity in his films proves the importance of cultural specificity, as he weaves local languages i.e.

Meitei, customs, and rituals into the framework of his storytelling. This commitment not only brings depth to his narratives but also shows the unique cultural landscape of the region. Pabung's emphasis on everyday life is particularly gripping. By focusing on the ordinary experiences of his characters, he draws the essence of human existence in its multitude forms. His films reveal that profound stories can emerge from the quiet moments of life, showcasing the struggles and triumphs of ordinary people. This approach cultivates a sense of connection that makes audiences t see their own experiences mirrored in the lives of his characters.

The aesthetic choices Pabung makes enrich his narrative technique. His minimalist approach to cinematography, coupled with a focus on capturing the beauty of the natural world, complements his storytelling. His films stand out for their poetic beauty, cultural specificity, and profound exploration of the human experience.

Pabung expresses his deep connection to the cultural landscape of Manipur through his films, which reflect the distinct identity known as "Manipuriness." This concept, as he articulates in the documentary *Laparoscopic Cinemascapes* by Joshy Joseph, involves the rich cultural heritage, traditions, and emotional nuances of Manipur, reflecting a vibrant ethos that permeates his work.

Pabung Aribam states in the documentary, *Laparoscopic Cinemascapes* (In Chapter-01, A cultural

Vortex), "This place Manipur, if you see, if you want to understand Manipuri culture… they created music, beautiful music, traditional music, folk music." Here, the emphasis on music and dance illustrates the integral role these forms of art play in shaping Manipuri identity. The mention of "Khongjom Parba", a poignant ballad commemorating the defeat of the Manipuri army in 1891, highlights not just a historical event, but also the way such narratives forge a collective memory and national pride. Delving into the realm of dance, Aribam refers to "Lai Haraoba", a ritualistic celebration showcasing the creation myths and spiritual symbolism intrinsic to Manipuri culture. He notes, "Dance means Lai Haraoba…everything is explained through dance and music." This emphasizes the idea that cultural expressions—be they through song, dance, or narrative—are not merely entertainment, but are imbued with profound meanings about existence, creation, and the human condition. His acknowledgment of the subtleties inherent in the "Raas" dance, symbolizing the union between the individual soul and the divine, further exemplifies the depths of Manipuri spirituality. Aribam reflects on how these forms of art have persisted through the ages despite the relatively small population of Manipur, asserting, "Imagine the talent."

Through these reflections, it becomes clear that his films act as vessels for preserving and amplifying the essence of Manipuriness. His storytelling, grounded in cultural specificity, reveals a deep emotional and spiritual introspection, challenging audiences to appreciate the delicate interplay of history, art, and identity.

Pabung Aribam says, "I make film in Manipuri" (personal communication, April 30, 2019) which suggests a profound exploration of the relationship between language, culture, and film. His perspective is rooted in the belief that language is not merely a medium of communication but a vessel for cultural identity. For Pabung Aribam, cinema, while often regarded as a universal form of art, should predominantly reflect the specific cultural nuances inherent in local languages. He critiques the overemphasis on technical demands from filmmaking crews, which he believes can weaken the authenticity of cultural expressions essential to Manipuri cinema. In his view, the cinematic experience should embody the subtleties of culture rather than conform to external market pressures and mainstream ideologies.

Pabung states that the art of acting in Manipuri cinema is distinctively different from practices prevalent in dominant film industries such as Bollywood. He draws our attention to how facial expressions are used in different cultural contexts. In Bollywood or other parts of India, emotional expressions are heavily codified, with actors using exaggerated facial movements to convey feelings. Conversely, the traditional art forms of Manipuri culture, such as Manipuri *Raas Leela*, focus on the broader body movements as the primary means of emotion expression. He articulates a stark contrast when discussing the expectations of actors in the Manipuri context. While mainstream cinema encourages a direct and intense eye contact with the camera for emotional depth, in Manipuri social norms, showing direct eye contact, especially with elders, is often considered disrespectful. In Manipur, one is taught to lower their gaze as an expression of respect. In film, however, actors are frequently instructed to look directly into the camera, leading Pabung Aribam to adamantly assert that this practice should not be adopted in the North-East.

In his film *Ishanou*, Aribam brilliantly illustrates his conviction that authentic emotional portrayal transcends conventional displays of sadness or joy. Rather than relying solely on visual cues such as tears, he emphasizes the raw, unscripted moments that actors capture during performances. For example, in the last scene of his film, *Ishanou*, an actress powerfully conveys grief during a separation scene, not through noticeable tears, but through the subtleties of body language and restrained expression. For Pabung Aribam, these unscripted moments of vulnerability offer a truer reflection of human emotion. Through his approach, he challenges the prevailing notion that emotion must be visually pronounced to be valid; he posits that authenticity can be found in the unsaid.

The scene in *Ishanou*, where the catfish is shown plays a crucial role in the dramatic progression of the story within the film. In this scene, we see

Tampha start to act strangely, which suggests she is on the path to becoming Maibi. The audience notices Tampha is already in the kitchen when Angoubi walks in with a bundle of catfish. When the bundle is opened and the fish. thrown onto the floor, they start wriggling everywhere. Tampha screams in fear and runs to her bed; Angoubi, Tampha's mother confused by Tampha's reaction, follows her. This moment is important because it reveals Tampha's inner struggle and hints at her future. The kitchen, typically a place of comfort, becomes unsettling for Tampha. Angoubi's puzzled expression shows she doesn't understand the depth of Tampha's fear. This scene marks the beginning of Tampha's transformation and suggests her new life. The wriggling fish represent life and change, contrasting with Tampha's fear and suggesting the bigger themes of identity and transformation in the story.

The final scene of the film exquisitely paints the film's main themes of family, love, and identity. Set at a shrine in Jiribam, a symbol of Manipuri culture, the scene portrays the feelings and relationships between Dhanabir, Tampha, and their daughter Bembem. The four young girls dancing represent the innocence and fragility of childhood, while Dhanabir and Tampha's hesitant exchanges show the unspoken emotions in their troubled relationship. Tampha's repeated questions, "Isn't she our Bembem, our daughter?" and "Does Bembem know that her mother… I am still alive?" express the pain and longing felt during their separation. Dhanabir's reluctance to speak, often responding with only silence or short answers, shows deeper cultural attitudes toward communication and emotion among Manipuris. Tampha's acceptance of Dhanabir's small nod reflects a heart-breaking sense of self-sacrifice and the cost of love. When she says "it's better she remains unaware of my existence as mother," it shows her deep resignation and the painful decisions that come with true love. As the scene progresses, Tampha becomes a tragic character, weighed down by her choices and her feelings of isolation grow stronger.

The moment becomes painfully poignant when Bembem unknowingly bows to Tampha, reflecting the emotional distance that separates them. As Tampha watches, Dhanabir and the girls walk slowly away, leaving her behind, an image filled with sadness and longing. Tampha stays behind and slowly walks back to the shrine. In the background, another Maibi is performing a traditional song called "Kanglei Thokpa," from the Lai Haraoba festival. The Maibi then sings a heart-wrenching lament: "Shining daughter of noble birth...I can't see her anymore... My Ishanou."

These moving words express the sentimental nature of love, a deep longing for connection, but also acknowledging the limits set by society and circumstances. The film's final scene offers a thoughtful reflection on family love and cultural identity, leaving viewers with a lasting emotional impact.

Reflecting on the challenges he faced while casting the role of Tampha as a Maibi, Pabung Aribam recounts that no artists from the Meitei community were willing to take on this role in the dance. In a surprising turn, he discovered an artist who, despite being a Brahmin, expressed a desire to embody the character of a Maibi (personal communication, April 30, 2022).

Pabung reflects on his journey as both an actor and a director, often asserting that the expression of emotions like anger is not standardized but instead highly subjective and culturally specific. Rather than yielding to popular formats that characterize other film industries, he advocates for an exploration of emotional articulation that coheres with local customs and traditions. This approach adopts an artistic identity unique to Manipuri cinema, one that honors its traditions while engaging with contemporary themes. By invoking the importance of authenticity, he affirms the need for a coherent narrative that respects the roots of cultural expression, advocating for a filmic language that honors the traditions, stories, and values of Manipuri society.

Pabung Aribam speaks passionately about his experiences as an actor, particularly reflecting on his role as a father in the groundbreaking first Manipuri cinema, *Matamgi Manipur*. He points out that acting is not just about delivering lines; it involves a deeper understanding of one's cultural expressions and emotional cues. For instance, he references the ancient

Indian text, the *Natyashastra*, which discusses various methods of portraying emotions. Traditionally, in many parts of India, expressing anger might involve broad gestures like opening one's eyes wide and raising one's voice. However, Pabung notes that in the North-Eastern region, there is a distinct approach. When someone gets angry, instead of widening their eyes and shouting, they often do the opposite— they might close their eyes. This subtle form of expression can carry its own weight; Pabung humorously warns, "If someone looks angry and begins to close their eyes, be careful— they might just hit you." This twist on emotional expression is a powerful sign to the region's unique cultural identity.

Pabung argues that rather than adhering to a one-size-fits-all approach from mainstream cinema, there should be a celebration of regional expressions. The diversity in acting methods, reflecting local customs and emotions, should be embraced and showcased. He takes pride in this individuality, asserting that by cherishing their unique ways of expression, artists from the northeast can carve out their own place in the cinematic landscape. This pride in cultural identity is not merely a call to action for actors but a broader declaration of respect for the rich traditions and practices that shape their art.

He articulates the thematic essence of the documentary *The Orchids of Manipur*, which explores the intricate relationship between Manipuri legends and the enthralling beauty of orchid flowers. Within this cinematic framework, the flowers are portrayed as engaging in a dance that is harmoniously intertwined with Manipuri music. This synergy is enriched by the filmmaker's technique of editing the shots to align with the fluid movements of the flowers. The varied colours of the orchids play a crucial role, that focus on the vibrancy and cultural significance of the visual narrative (personal communication, 2016).

I want to point out two scenes from the film *Imagi Ningthem* to show what makes Pabung a great filmmaker and how rich the film is in visuals and music. These scenes really stand out and reveal his exceptional skills and storytelling style. In the first sequence, we witness a transformative moment in the lives of the characters. Gandhar informs the grandfather about an important revelation: Thoithoi's biological father and Ekashini's intention to adopt him. This moment is pivotal and loaded with emotion. The grandfather is faced with the prospect of change. The filmmaker captures this moment with a close-up shot of the grandfather's face. Here, audience can see an expression of pure, unarticulated joy. The close-up effectively conveys a depth of feeling that words cannot express. What makes this moment even more powerful is the sense of joy that radiates from the grandfather. We see his eyes light up with happiness, a look that conveys not just his delight at the news but also his love for Thoithoi. This simple yet profound expression demonstrates the strong bond between the grandfather and Thoithoi.

As the close-up of the grandfather fades, the scene transitions to a long sequence featuring Thoithoi flying a kite in the courtyard. The kite, a colourful symbol of childhood joy, becomes the centrepiece of this moment. With a bamboo stick in hand, Thoithoi runs through the courtyard, his laughter echoing against the backdrop of the sky. This sequence is visually striking, filled with vibrant colours and the carefree energy of a child at play.

The act of kite flying is not merely a playful activity; it is a potent symbol in this context. In many cultures, flying a kite represents freedom, hope, and the aspiration to rise above challenges. For the grandfather, watching Thoithoi fly the kite signifies his joyful acceptance of the changes in their lives. It reflects the joy that comes from seeing a loved one experience happiness. In contrast, for Thoithoi, the kite represents his innocence and untroubled spirit as he observes the changes around him. The sequence strikingly captures the essence of childhood, where simple pleasures bring immense joy and laughter. The kite takes flight, soaring high in the air, signifying the hope and possibilities that lie ahead for Thoithoi and his grandfather. It conveys the idea that, despite life's complexities, there is beauty in the small moments of joy that one can find, especially in the innocence of childhood.

The second sequence unfolds when Ekashini comes to visit Thoithoi. This moment carries its own emotional weight, as the arrival of Thoithoi's mother signifies a reunion filled with anticipation and excitement. Here, we see Pishak, a young girl and Thoithoi's friend, bursting with excitement. She rushes to tell Thoithoi the news, prompting a feeling of eagerness and urgency. As soon as Thoithoi hears that his mother has come, the two children take off running through their village. This moment is visualised beautifully as they race through the green paddy fields, the dried rivulet, and narrow pathways of the village. Their laughter and excitement are noticeable and we as audience are drawn into this joyful chase. This running scene is not just about physical movement but is filled with symbolic significance. The rush of Pishak and Thoithoi through the landscape depicts childhood innocence and the unfiltered joy of friendship. Their experience of running through nature is a celebration of life, and the vibrant imagery serves to heighten the emotional impact of the moment.

The second sequence reminds me of Durga-Apu's running scene in Satyajit Ray's *Pather Pachali* (1955). In Indian cinema, the interplay of motifs such as the train and the mother acts as a profound commentary on childhood, and the nature of human relationships. In *Imagi Ningthem*, the scene where Pishak and Thoithoi run through their village personifies the exuberance of youth, drawing the essence of wonder and discovery.

The running scene in Satyajit Ray's *Pather Panchali* (1955) where Apu and Durga-Apu chase after the train, is a moment that stands out as a master class in visual storytelling. The scene is a masterful example of how a simple action can convey the emotional complexity of a moment. The train, a distant symbol of an unknown world, represents freedom, adventure, and the infinite possibilities of the outside world. For Apu and Durga-Apu, the train is a source of wonder and curiosity, evoking a sense of awe and trepidation. The train in *Pather Panchali* is a powerful symbol of the unknown, representing aspirations and dreams that extend beyond the immediate and familiar. For Durga and Apu, the train signifies a world they have yet to experience, filled with mystery and excitement. They run through the Kaashi field to have a peep of the train, in fact, for them, train is a symbol of unknown world, never seen before how it looks like. Their race towards it is not just a physical act but also an emotional journey, a quest for understanding and connection with a broader reality. The train embodies both a longing for adventure and the stark contrast of their rural existence, highlighting the tension between their innocent desires and the harsh realities of life.

In fact, the use of the word "mother" as a motif in *Imagi Ningthem* is reminiscent of the train in *Pather Panchali*. Both are symbols of a world beyond the confines of the village, a world that represents freedom, joy, and possibility. However, while the train is a distant, almost mythical concept, Ekashini is a tangible, living presence in the life of Thoithoi and Pishak. The running sequence towards Ekashini is therefore a more intimate and emotional experience, conveying the deep bond between the children and their mother. Both motifs, the train and the mother, juxtapose the themes of desire for exploration and the emotional ties that ground us. While the train represents the allure of the unknown, the mother signifies connection and safety. Pabung Aribam reflects that Thoithoi's longing for his mother mirrors his own childhood experience of losing his mother at a young age in one way or another.

I always look at the film *Imagi Ningthem* as the *Pather Panchali* of Manipuri cinema, not just for its striking visual sequences but also for its innovative narrative techniques. Pabung's approach celebrates the richness of local culture while addressing universal themes, that effectively rewrite the narrative possibilities within Manipuri filmmaking.

His documentary titled *Yelhou Jagoi: The Dances of Yelhou Jagoi* for the Indira Gandhi National Centre for the Arts (IGNCA) in New Delhi. The documentary aimed to showcase the traditional dance form of Yelhou Jagoi, which is an important part of the culture and heritage of Manipur. His approach to making the documentary was unique. He chose not to include any commentary, narration, or voiceover in the film. He wanted the audience to experience the dance form in its purest and most authentic form, without any external explanations or interpretations. This decision was deliberate and intentional, as he believed that the beauty and significance of Yelhou Jagoi should speak for itself. When he presented the film to officials and scholars at the IGNCA, they suggested that he should add narration or commentary to make the film more accessible and engaging for a wider audience. However, he stood firm in his decision. He believed that the complexity and richness of 'Yelhou Jagoi' would be lost if he added commentary. Instead, he wanted audience to be able to appreciate the dance form on its own merits, without any preconceptions or biases. His approach was a bold and innovative one. In doing so, Pabung was able to showcase the beauty and significance of 'Yelhou Jagoi' in a way that was both authentic and engaging.

Let us examine the opening sequence of the film *Sanabi* (The Grey Pony). The film begins with a wide shot, capturing a solitary figure on a bicycle positioned centrally in the frame, framed against the backdrop of a majestic mountain. Wisps of stubble smoke rise gently in the air, enhancing the scene's atmosphere. As the camera slowly pans to follow the figure, it gradually becomes evident that the subject is moving away, eventually framing out of the shot. In the subsequent scene, the figure re-enters the frame, now in motion on the bicycle, accompanied by the sight of a bullock cart passing by. A mid-close-up shot reveals that the cyclist is an elderly Manipuri woman, attired in a traditional phanek and shawl. The next immediate shot depicts her dismounting the bicycle to navigate a fragile bridge, carefully walking while holding the cycle. What truly elevates this sequence is filmmaker Pabung Aribam's use of ambient sound, particularly the creaking of the bicycle, which immerses the viewer in the tranquillity of village life in Manipur. The absence of musical accompaniment enhances the authenticity of the scene. It allows the natural sounds to resonate and convey the beauty of the setting. This creative choice reflects the Pabung's poetic vision. Indeed, Pabung Aribam could rightly be described as a poet of cinema for the lyrical and rhythmic beauty of his film.

In the film *Leipaklei*, filmmaker Pabung Aribam adroitly uses colour to poignantly reflect the protagonist's psychological state. The character Leipaklei, once married but ultimately abandoned by her husband for a woman from Mokokchung, faces profound loneliness as she returns to her parents' land, now empty in their absence. Their passing leaves her in a challenging situation, raising her daughter and managing a shop to support them both. Adding to her sorrow, Leipaklei's first love, Ibotomba is believed to have perished in the war, having never returned home. Against this backdrop of grief and melancholy, Leipaklei's costume choices are particularly symbolic. Throughout the film, she predominantly wears muted, faded colours that convey her despair and emotional turmoil. In contrast, during flashback scenes that evoke happier moments, one showcasing her bridal attire and another highlighting happy times with her boyfriend, Ibotomba, she is adorned in vibrant hues. This shift in her clothing signifies the stark contrast between her past happiness and present sorrow. Frequently, she is seen in a white *innaphi* with check patterns and a soft pink *phanek* costumes that reflect her subdued existence rather than one filled with brightness. Leishangthem Tonthoi, who portrays Leipaklei, shares her insights, noting that Pabung is meticulous about her costumes. She explains, "As I am an abandoned lady, but not a widow, my psychological position is different, therefore, Pabung chose somewhat dull-coloured costumes for me." This careful consideration of costuming not only enriches the film's visual narrative but also deepens the audience's understanding of Leipaklei's complex emotional landscape.

One of the most exquisite and symbolically rich scenes in the film, deeply imbued with metaphorical significance through the character of Leipaklei, unfolds when Leipaklei is reunited with her boyfriend, who was presumed dead. As he returns to the village and reassures her of his commitment to stay, the scene is set before a dusty mirror, which symbolises reflection and renewal. In a beautifully composed close-up shot, we witness Leipaklei gently cleaning the mirror with her hand, a gesture that indicates her desire to clear away the past and embrace the present. She then adorns herself with a *nachom*, a delicate flower (Leipaklei uses *Takhellei* (butterfly ginger lily), placing it gracefully in the upper part of her ear. This suggests hope and new beginnings. The scene opens in silence, intensifying the emotional gravity of the moment. As she fixes the *nachom* in her hair, music softly begins to play in the background. A soft smile gradually emerges on her face, reflecting a sense of joy and relief. Pabung dexterously zooms in to capture the intricacies of her expression through an extreme close-up, and it displays her profound transformation.

Pabung interconnects cultural authenticity with a humanistic approach to storytelling. His adherence to a linear narrative structure is an effective device that facilitates clarity and emotional resonance. At the heart of his cinematic philosophy is a profound understanding of humanity, a quality that transcends conventional binaries of good and evil. Instead of focusing on moral dichotomies, he explores the intricacies of human relationships. This perspective echoes the cultural ethos of Manipuri society, which often embraces a more holistic view of human nature. His films are deeply intertwined with Manipuri culture, language, and music, which he uses as both a narrative device and a means of enriching the emotional landscape of his stories. The integration of traditional Manipuri music not only enhances the audio-visual experience but also reinforces cultural identity. This synergy between cultural elements and human emotions is a hallmark of his work and distinguishes him in a landscape often dominated by form over substance.

In an industry often characterized by spectacle and superficiality, Pabung's filmmaking emerges as a refreshing reminder of the power of storytelling rooted to cultural authenticity and emotional depth. His legacy will undoubtedly inspire upcoming generations of filmmakers to embrace the richness of content and the intimate complexities of the human spirit.

***

Chapter Seven

The Political Heart Behind the Lens

Ewa Mazierska, professor of contemporary cinema at the University of Central Lancashire, discusses the complexities of "political cinema" in her article, "Introduction: Marking Political Cinema," published in Framework: The Journal of Cinema and Media (January 2014). She acknowledges the challenges in defining the concept of "political cinema," emphasizing that, following Karl Marx's assertion that cultural products reflect their production conditions, both material and ideological, and drawing on Ludwig Wittgenstein's idea that language shapes reality, the prevailing view is that "all films are political." This perspective suggests that films, whether intentionally or unintentionally, either embrace or contradict a given view of the world.

Prof. Mazierska argues that perhaps the best-known definition was offered by Jean-Luc Godard during his "militant period," when he announced that he did not just want to make "political films," but to make them "politically." In his case, this meant making films in a self-reflexive way, revealing the means of their production and directly engaging with the audience, for example, by showing them in factories and during rallies for the purpose of politicizing the viewers.

Prof. Mazierska quotes Mike Wayne, who defines political films as those that "in one way or another address unequal access to and distribution of material and cultural resources, and the hierarchies of legitimacy and status accorded to those differentials." She has mentioned that, although in theory we accept that "all films are political," in practice, mainly marked and oppositional films are singled out for discussions of politics in film. She has argued that marking films as political is always historically and culturally specific. Some films that were regarded as highly political when they were made lost their political appeal over time as the causes for which they fought became obsolete. For other films, this shift occurred when they travelled from one country to another. Conversely, although it happens more rarely, films regarded as neutral in relation to politics during their heyday might be recognized as political by new generations of viewers.

In the context of Pabung Aribam, while some may argue that he has not explicitly focused on "political" films, Prof. Mazierskas arguments challenge this notion. Pabung is far from being apolitical, both as a filmmaker and as an engaged citizen. As a filmmaker, he uses his voice to address critical issues through his film, and as a citizen, he actively protests when the Manipuri identity is under threat.

I would like to refer the film *Paokhum Ama* as a significant political work, as it critiques and questions the role of government and its policies while portraying the disillusionment of the younger generation that results in their turning to violence. In a personal conversation, Pabung Aribam described *Paokhum Ama* as his political film. His approach to cinema reflects a nuanced understanding of the intersection between cultural narratives and political realities. In *Paokhum Ama*, Pabung not only critiques government policies but also draws the sentiments of disillusioned youth, that weaves together a complex mosaic of personal and collective experiences. This film acts as a vital commentary on the socio-political landscape, that shows the frustrations and aspirations of a generation increasingly alienated from those in power. By framing his work within the context of cultural identity, Pabung illustrates how politics is inseparably linked to the lived experiences of individuals. His film *Paokhum Ama* is a proof to his commitment to exploring the complexities of human existence within a political framework that challenges the notion that his films do not explicitly address the political sphere.

His engagement with political issues extends well beyond the confines of his films. His active participation in protests, such as those against the Armed Forces (Special Powers) Act (AFSPA) and his symbolic gesture of returning the Padma Shri award during the Citizenship Amendment Act (CAA) movement, elucidate his political consciousness. These acts of protest are not simply reactions to immediate political crises; they represent his unwavering commitment to justice and the well-being of his community.

This brings to light an essential dichotomy within Pabung's work: the relationship between cultural specificity and political consciousness. By prioritizing cultural narratives, he cultivates a space where the richness of Manipuri identity can emerge, often revealing the original socio-political nuances. The cultural narratives he offers can be interpreted as implicit commentaries on the political struggles and aspirations of the Manipuri people. For instance, themes of displacement, identity crises, and communal narratives in his films mirror the broader socio-political landscape marked by insurgency, resistance, and a quest for autonomy.

On February 3, 2019, Pabung made a significant announcement regarding his decision to return the Padma Shri award--the fourth highest civilian award in India-- he received in recognition of his contributions to Indian cinema. This gesture was positioned as an act of solidarity with the widespread public protests occurring in response to the Citizenship (Amendment) Bill (CAB) of 2016, a controversial legislative proposal that has sparked intense debate across various regions in India, particularly in the northeastern states. In his address to reporters at his residence in Imphal, he articulated the deep concerns and sentiments prevalent among the people of Manipur and the broader North-Eastern region. His declaration was not merely an artist's stance but a reflection of the collective anxiety regarding the perceived marginalization of the North-Eastern states within the larger political framework of India. Aribam's assertion that "the people in Manipur need protection" underscores the existential fears about identity, demographics, and resource allocation facing the region, particularly in light of the socio-political transformations engendered by the CAB. His critical examination of political representation highlighted a systemic issue: "the state has only one or two MPs in a house of 500 plus members." This statement underscores the stark reality of political underrepresentation that the North-Eastern states endure in the Indian Parliament. By questioning, "what voice can the northeast have in Parliament," Aribam articulates a broader concern regarding the efficacy of democratic representation and the consequent implications for the rights and voices of marginalized communities. The CAB, which seeks to provide a pathway to Indian citizenship for certain religious minorities fleeing persecution from neighboring countries, has been contested for its perceived discriminatory provisions that ostensibly exclude Muslims. Critics argue that such exclusions foster a climate of fear and insecurity, particularly in regions with rich ethnic and cultural diversity such as Manipur. Aribam's return of the Padma Shri thus emerges as a poignant critique of policies that can potentially exacerbate societal fractures and undermine the inclusive tenets of Indian democracy. Filmmaker Aribam says to the reporters, "They should respect us as a state, small or big. It should not be counted on a population basis. I raise this because the Union of India is made up of states," he said. "When the northeastern states jointly represent or present something to the government, they should consider it, and if they do not consider it, naturally we have to oppose. So, as part of showing solidarity, I decided to return the award" (Samom, 2019).

Again, Pabung said, "The Bill is against the interests of the people of North-East and the indigenous people of Manipur. Several people here (Manipur) have opposed the Bill, but it seems they (the Central government) are determined to pass it. Padma Shri is an honor; it is one of the highest forms of recognition in India. So, I thought the best way to protest was by returning it." He added, "There is no protection for the people of the valley (in Manipur). If more people come, then they (the indigenous people) will vanish in the valley or hills. What's the point of having culture if there are no indigenous people? Manipuri's future will be all diluted. Northeast is becoming a dumping ground" (IANS, 2019). Here, Pabung Aribam's statement reveals several philosophical footings. His opposition to the bill and concern for the indigenous people of Manipur indicate a decolonial stance, critiquing the legacy of colonialism that continues to affect marginalized communities. By emphasizing the vulnerability of indigenous peoples and the cultural homogenization that would result from the bill, Pabunng embodies principles focused on resisting colonial influences metaphorically.

His advocacy for the rights of indigenous populations highlights a commitment to the philosophy that affirms the necessity of recognizing and respecting the land, culture, and autonomy of these communities. His assertion that "Manipur's future will be all diluted" reflects a critique of modernity, suggesting that the influx of outsiders threatens to destroy the unique cultural identity of the Manipuri people. Aribam's emphasis on protecting indigenous culture towards its survival suggests a leaning toward cultural relativism, which values all cultures equally and advocates for their recognition. His poignant action of returning the Padma Shri award serves as a form of non-violent resistance. This symbolic gesture draws attention to his beliefs and concerns regarding the bill, revealing his commitment to peaceful protest as a means to voice dissent.

It is worth considering the aesthetic choices that Pabung Aribam employs in his films – the use of local dialects, traditional music, and rituals – which not only anchor his works in their cultural context but also works as a political statement of authenticity and resistance against the homogenization of identity. His commitment to portraying the richness of Manipuri culture is a quiet yet profound resistance against a backdrop of political marginalization.

It would be incorrect to claim that Pabung does not make political films. My arguments clearly show that Pabung Aribam indeed engages with political cinema, and his work reflects a strong stance on art, life, and the political landscape. As a filmmaker, Pabung is a deep thinker, and his philosophy reveals an understanding of the relationship between culture and politics. His activism outside of filmmaking, clarifies through his active participation in political movements of his state, strengthens his role as a politically conscious filmmaker who uses his platform to advocate for his community. I believe his legacy goes beyond the films he has made. It lies in his commitment to the cultural and political awareness of his homeland, Manipur, an advocacy that echoes powerfully both within and beyond the world of cinema.

Works Cited

IANS. (2019, February 3). Manipuri filmmaker Aribam Syam Sharma to return Padma Shri in protest against Citizenship Bill. *https://www.indiatvnews.com.* https://www.indiatvnews.com/entertainment/regional-cinema-manipuri-filmmaker-aribam-syam-sharma-to-return-padma-shri-in-protest-against-citizenship-bill-502613

Samom, S. (2019, February 3). Renowned Manipuri filmmaker returns Padma Shri to protest Citizenship Bill. *Hindustan Times.* https://www.hindustantimes.com/india-news/renowned-manipuri-filmmaker-returns-padma-shri-to-protest-citizenship-bill/story-7FL7zNg3cFVyJQJTdOHLkI.html

Mazierska, Ewa. "Introduction: Marking Political Cinema." Framework The Journal of Cinema and Media 55(1) 2014. DOI:10.13110/framework.55.1.0033.

https://www.researchgate.net/publication/305756380_Introduction_Marking_Political_Cinema.

Epilogue

Pabung Aribam is not only a legendary figure in Indian cinema but also a pioneering force in the field of theatre and music in Manipur. His extensive contributions to theatre and music have left an indelible mark on the cultural landscape of the region. When observing Pabung's legacy, it is essential to consider his influence on both theatre and music in equal measure, as they are intricately linked in his body of work. In recent years, there has been a notable resurgence of interest in his contributions, particularly within the context of Manipuri theatre and music. This renewed appreciation reflects a growing recognition of his approaches and the depth of his creativity. As scholars and enthusiasts explore his works, they find the profound impact he has had on shaping the artistic identity of Manipur.

In the article "Manipuri Theatre: Past and Present," Khongul Liklam notes the foundational contributions of key figures in Manipuri theatre, particularly Maharaj Kumari Binodini Devi and Aribam Syam Sharma. As Liklam writes: "In fields of Manipuri Theatre and Cinema, both Maharaj Kumari Binodini Devi and Aribam Syam Sharma are pioneers. The renowned absurdist playwright of Manipur, Late Shri Biren expressed in no uncertain terms the foundational contributions of Aribam Syam Sharma to the development and direction that Manipuri

Theatre took. "If not for the realist plays that *Oja* (referring to Aribam Syam Sharma) directed, the evolution of Manipuri Theatre would have been slower. When he took up my three plays *Khongchat*, *Hallakpa*, and *Ani* for direction, his approach to directing them was unimaginably different. These productions were characterized by critics as absurdist plays, but I would take these directions as 'dramatisation of a poetic vision'. *Oja*'s visualisation of my poetic vision must have taken tremendous artistic effort. If anyone attempts a history of Manipuri theatre, it is imperative that *Oja* Syam be given his due. If not, then there shall be an irremediable gap in that history, it shall remain incomplete."

In the tumultuous socio-political landscape of 1960s Manipur, marked by a mass student uprising against the government over food insecurity, Maharaj Kumari Binodini Devi penned the play *Ashangba Nongjabi*. As noted by Chingtham (May 5, 2025): "The Syam Sharma of those times, along with the artists of *Roop Raag*, performed the play. The social injustices, the exploitation of the weak by the strong, and the scourge of unemployment- the hues and colours they took in the minds and hearts of the people, could not be washed away by the new reality of an Independent Manipur, then merged with India. The youth of the urban middle class Manipur was a dejected lot. What was the purpose of their existence? Was their life waiting for the curtain to fall? These questions descended on them. This was the ground on which *Ashangbe Nongjabi* (Azure Clouds of a Crimson

Evening) germinated. This was the crucible in which the character of Gautam in the play was forged. He represented the youths who harboured the disquiet of the times they carried within."

Chingtham (2025) elaborates that *Ashangba Nongjabi*, rich in layers of meaning and analysis, was directed by one of our pioneering experimental theatre directors, Aribam Syam Sharma, and produced by the cultural/theatre group *Roop Raag*. Though the genre of the production is close to that of the realistic play, the intrusion of unconventional characters and style also signals the possibility of classifying it as experimental.

Also, Chingtham emphasises that "Apart from the absurdist plays of Shri Biren, Aribam Syam Sharma directed absurdist works from both the West and India, notably those of Badal Sircar."

Regarding Pabung's innovative acting style introduced inn Manipuri theatre through the direction of this play, *Ashangbe Nongjabi,* E. Nila Kanta Singh writes in *The Manipuri Times* (n.d.), " Entirely original in concept and in the art of acting style (Director: Syam Sharma), this play opens a new world of beauty on the Manipuri stage which keeps in tune with the changing styles of theatre…It is indeed an experience to watch for the first time, perhaps in Manipur, a deeply psychological play with new horizon of contemporary acting style."

Lamago quotes Pabung Aribam in his article, *Manipuri Matam Esheida Aribam Syam Sharmagi Khudol*

(The Contributions of Aribam Syam Sharma to Manipuri Contemporary (Modern) Music), as published in *Poknapham*, May 10, 2025. Pabung says, "When I compose, I look for inspiration from traditional music's elements to create something new. I would therefore advise future directors to experiment with this as a viable approach." Lamago asserts that 'in recognition of his lifelong association with Manipuri music since he was in school (Class 9) when he composed his first song, for the immeasurable and pioneering works in the the field, and for his dedication, the Manipur Sahitya Parishad conferred him its highest honour in the field *Sangeet Ratna* (Modern Music). There is no element of doubt that in the movement that made Modern Manipuri Music an independent art form, in its separation from stage and proscenium theatre, the artist's position rests as one of the forerunners.'

Pabung's engagement with music represents a profound and transformative journey that began in his formative years. His introduction to the world of music can be traced back to his childhood, specifically through his initial music lessons at the Johnstone School. This early exposure to music education not only kindled his passion for the art form but also served as a crucial stepping stone in his creative development. It was during this period that Pabung composed his debut song, *Khammu Khammu Mitki Pirang*, when he was in the ninth grade, in 1952.

Upon his enrollment at D.M. College of Sciences, his artistic course expanded further, interconnecting with his growing interest in theater. In collaboration with fellow enthusiasts including Phulendra, Samarendra, Pahari, Rabindra, and Aken, he co-founded the Amateur Artiste Association. This collective emerged as a vital moment for innovative music and drama.

Lamago (May 17, 2025) writes: "After his matriculation (he stood 3rd in the state-level examination), he studied science in DM college. As if it was fated, here he met individuals who loved music and theatre like Nongmaithem Pahari, Arambam Samarinda, Khuraijam Phulendra, Ningthoujam Akendra and others. This encounter was to become an important event for a turn in Manipuri music. College life was a series of musical and theatrical productions and performances. He was elected social and cultural secretary. He and his friends studied music with Oja Mutum Madhu of Sagaloband. They formed the group "A Cube" (Amateur Artists Association). Gurumayum Rabindra Sharma and some others also joined the group. It came to prominence within a short period. It produced and performed landmark songs like *Anouba Jugki Anouba Asha Puduna*, *Kayam Watli Lamdam Do*, *Unarakta Lotlibi Leirang Nangbu Sathouro* (all three composed by Aribam Syam Sharma). Many well-received plays were also produced by A Cube.

The activities of the Amateur Artiste Association were not merely confined to the composition of music; they extended to dynamic performances that showcased theatrical productions and concerts across various state and university settings. Pabung's rising fame as a vocalist led to numerous invitations to perform in local venues, where his innovative compositions found a receptive audience. The intimate settings of traditional courtyards, known as "Shumang," became a backdrop for the sharing of his works. The efforts of the Amateur Artiste Association laid the foundational groundwork for *Roop Raag*, a pioneering musical institution that emerged as an example of artistic excellence."

Pabung undertook an extensive and multidisciplinary education at Visva-Bharati, Santiniketan. His studies encompassed both Rabindra Sangeet and Philosophy. For four years, he dedicated himself to the intricate art of Rabindra Sangeet, a genre of music that encapsulates the poetic and philosophical essence of the works of the renowned Bengali polymath, Rabindranath Tagore. Under the guidance of distinguished mentors such as Shantidev Ghosh and Konika Banerjee, both highly respected figures in the realm of Rabindra Sangeet, Pabung honed his artistic sensibilities. During this process, he discovered that Tagore's music addresses a multitude of themes, ranging from love and nature to existential inquiries and social issues. This thematic diversity not only captivated him but also illuminated the expansive potential of song writing as a form of artistic expression. He recognized that each piece of music could convey complex emotions and ideas. In addition to his focus on Rabindra Sangeet, Pabung studied Hindustani Classical Music. Through this combination of Rabindra Sangeet and Hindustani Classical Music, Pabung developed a nuanced appreciation for the depth and versatility of Indian music, eventually influencing his own creative pursuits and artistic voice.

In 1958, after finishing his undergraduate studies, Pabung Aribam had his first experience in a recording studio while heading home to Imphal. At that time, the Guwahati station of All India Radio (A.I.R) had just started a program for the Manipuri language. Seizing this opportunity, he auditioned and recorded seven of his earlier compositions. This marked the beginning of his long connection with A.I.R. The opening of the A.I.R station in Imphal in 1963 was a significant turn for Manipuri music. It provided a much-needed platform for Manipuri artists and helped spread this new style of music across the region. As one of the first officially recognized vocal artists, Pabung played a key role in this movement.

As a singer, he recorded these songs: 1) *Thaja Epal Langlibi;* 2) *Thaja Mabu Pamjaruba;* 3) *Thamoi Pandrabi Kanagi Murtida;* 4) *Ningamdraba Eigi Thamoina;* 5) *Shamu Macha Ama;* 6) *Nungsidaba Natte Nangbu;* 7) *Kanagi Leikolda Shatpino;* 8) *Jwar Karakle;* 9) *Taibang Keithel Karakpada;* 10) *Ningba Thungdraba Eise;* 11) *Kari Laiwa Yaobano.* Some of the most famous songs recorded on discs are: 1. *Kayam Watli Lamdamdo;* 2. *Unarakta Lotlibi Leirang Nangbu Shathouro;* 3. *Taibang*

Chinjak Chaduna; 4. *Ekaithibi Leirangi Mapokni;* 5. *Miraba Khonjelda Nungshiba Surda.* In the area of devotional music, he composer several significant works that hold a special place in the religious practices of the Manipuri Vaishnav community. These compositions include: 1. *Niti Leela* - a performance that reflects the moral and ethical teachings in devotional context. 2. *Gosht Leela* - This piece focuses on the playful and loving interactions of Lord Krishna with his devotees and friends. 3. *Goura Bhabhi* - A musical piece that highlights the devotion and love surrounding the figures in Vaishnavism. 4. *Nimai Sanyas* - A work that depicts the life of Nimai, another name for Lord Chaitanya, and his journey toward spiritual enlightenment. These compositions are not just musical performances; they are integral to the ritual life cycles of the Manipuri Vaishnav community, often performed during religious ceremonies, festivals, and important life events. In addition to these works, he also composed an epic musical piece called *Krishna Leela*, which is a grand production consisting of 30 episodes and lasts about 10 hours. This extensive work tells the story of Lord Krishna's life and journeys, and it was created for All India Radio (A.I.R.), showcasing the rich cultural heritage and devotional devotion in Manipuri music (PROFILE AS a SINGER | *FilmsofAribamSyam,* n.d.).

His contributions to music are noteworthy and among his significant works is the composition of the opening theme song for the 5th National Games, held in Imphal, titled *Ho Pari Sangai Nangbu.* This piece is not only a musical introduction to the event but also captures the spirit of unity and celebration within the community. He also composed a series of songs called *Laibak Phabi Kekrupat*, which honours the heroes who died in the June uprising of 2001. Additionally, he wrote songs about the life of the famous leader Hijam Irabot, and these songs were compiled into an album named *Miyamgi Luchingba Irabot.* For the 40th anniversary of A.I.R. Imphal, he composed two special songs: the opening song *Nongthang Meira Shadong Oina* and the closing song *He Pukning Tuktharaba Lao Nangbu Sida Lao*" (PROFILE AS a SINGER | *FilmsofAribamSyam,* n.d.).

Pabung beautifully composed the music for the Manipur state song, *Sana Leibak Manipur*, (Manipur, the Land of Gold) with heartfelt lyrics by Bachaspatimayum Jayantakumar Sharma. While the song was officially adopted as the state song on August 21, 2021, it had been cherished in unofficial use since 1967.

In addition to his extensive work in music composition, he also made significant contributions to the cinematic landscape by composing songs for various films. Among these, notable works include: 1) *Matamgi Manipur* (1972); 2) *Lamja Parshuram* (1974), a film that further established his reputation in the industry; 3) *Shaphabee* (1978), a project that proved his evolving artistry; 4) *Kombirei*, which added to his oeuvre (BOOKS | *FilmsofAribamSyam*, n.d.). The songs he composed for these films garnered substantial popularity.

Pabung also authored several books which includes *Living Shadows* (2006), an autobiographical work that offers a personal narrative of his experiences. In collaboration with Chongtham Kamala, he co-authored *Eshei Binodinigi* (Songs of Binodini, 2014), a comprehensive exploration of the songs written by the notable figure M.K. Binodini. Pabung Aribam's work *Manipuri Cinema: Eigi Paodam* (Manipuri Cinema: My Experiences from the Journey, 2016) provides a detailed account of the origins and evolution of Manipuri cinema. Together, these works show his commitment to documenting and interpreting cultural narratives in the context of both literature and film.

Pabung's impact on Manipuri music is marked by a series of significant contributions that span his roles as a composer, performer, and singer. His works not only catapult the status of Manipuri music but also spark a cultural renaissance that celebrated the rich artistic heritage of the region. In recognition of his extraordinary contributions to Modern Manipuri music, Pabung Aribam was honoured with the Sangeet Ratna by the Manipur Sahitya Parishad. Also, he was made a Fellow of the Manipur State Kala Akademi. His achievements have also been celebrated with the N. Pahari Memorial Lifetime Achievement Award, which recognizes his significant contributions to Manipuri modern music. The All Manipur Matam

Ishei Kanglup (AMMIK) has also bestowed upon him a lifetime achievement award. Beyond these accolades, Aribam has been honored with the Kamal Kumari National Award in the field of Art & Culture, and he is also a recipient of the prestigious Padmashri.

Note: *The quotations in this chapter by Buddha Chingtham and Lamago were originally written in Meitei. The articles and songs have been translated into English by Dr. Aribam Uttam Sharma, to whom I am deeply indebted.*

Works Cited

PROFILE AS A SINGER | FilmsofAribamSyam. (n.d.). FilmsofAribamSyam. https://aribamsyamarchives.wixsite.com/filmsofaribamsyam/profile-as-a-singer

BOOKS | FilmsofAribamSyam. (n.d.). FilmsofAribamSyam. https://aribamsyamarchives.wixsite.com/filmsofaribamsyam/books

In Conversation with Aribam Syam Sharma

Parthajit Baruah: Sir, what does cinema mean to you?

Aribam Syam Sharma: For me, it is just a medium to express my feelings, my emotions, and my reaction to a society. It is a sort of expression of my creative urge in me, just like music. I am a singer, I express in a particular medium of singing, the same way, film is a medium.

Parthajit Baruah: Can you tell us about your time at Viswa Bharati in Santiniketan and how it influenced your career in music and film?

Aribam Syam Sharma: I studied Philosophy and Rabindra Sangeet at Viswa Bharati in Santiniketan where I did my B.A and M.A. My first passion was music; I loved singing and composing, and I became the first Manipuri music director for Matamgi Manipur. While studying there, I also learned about philosophy, which influenced my views on art and life.

Parthajit Baruah: Which film had a strong effect on you, and why?

Aribam Syam Sharma: One film that really inspired me was *Ajantik*, by Ritwik Ghatak. I can't remember exactly when I saw it, but it was probably between 1956 and 1960. When I saw this particular film, there was something in me. Somehow, it gave me an impression that yes, this is a kind of film which I want to make.

Parthajit Baruah: Did *Ajantik* give you the determination to make your own film?

Aribam Syam Sharma: Yes, *Ajantik* inspired me a lot. At first, I wanted to make films that had social meaning. Back in 1972, in Manipur, there were many types of Hindi films. We felt pressure to make those kinds of films because they could bring in money. So, in 1974, I made *Lamja Parsuram*, followed by *Saaphabee* in 1976 and *Olangthagee Wangmadasoo* in 1979.

Parthajit Baruah: What challenges did you face regarding the survival of Manipuri cinema when you went back to Manipur?

Aribam Syam Sharma: I faced several challenges regarding the survival of Manipuri cinema, including the limited number of cinema houses available—only three or four—and the small audience for Manipuri language films. One might find it surprising that filmmaking was very expensive then, and there was practically no market for our films. Even then, they said, " Never try to make Manipuri Films. It is not possible." It was said by those who know about filmmaking and studying market. Films were distributed from Guwahati. Even they asked me to make a Hindi film. Distribution was primarily handled from Guwahati. Even though some of my acquaintances suggested I make Hindi films because I won national awards. But I made it clear that I wanted to make films in Manipuri. I believed it was essential to work in our own language.

Parthajit Baruah: What made you think you should make a film?

Aribam Syam Sharma: After the commercial success of my film *Olangthagee Wangmadasoo* that came out in 1979, I said that the time has come to make film on 'my own liking'. I also felt that Manipuri cinema could survive. Many other producers felt the same way. I saw that a lot of films used unnecessary things like songs and fight scenes, which are called "masala" films. So, I decided to make different kinds of films. I chose to stop making masala films and started focusing on more realistic and meaningful stories.

Parthajit Baruah: Sir, could you tell us a little about *Shaphabee?*

Aribam Syam Sharma: Let's talk about my film *Shaphabee.* We have a rich storytelling tradition in Manipur, and one of the first films to truly capture that on screen was *Shaphabee.* It is based on a very popular folk story, and it was the first Manipuri film to earn the Silver Lotus award. That was a huge achievement, a real turning point for us. Then there's *Matamgi Manipur*, where I worked as music director and also acted as father. Now, that film was the first to receive the National Merit Award. You might know it better as the National President's Award, as it was called back then.

Parthajit Baruah: Can you share a memorable incident from the filming of a film?

Aribam Syam Sharma: There's one day during the shooting of *Sanabi* that stands out vividly in my memory. As our crew, which included a number of non-Manipuri technicians, made their way to our filming location, an unexpected turn of events unfolded. As they came, they were abruptly stopped by the Central Reserve Police Force (CRPF). The soldiers commanded them to get down from their vehicle. I can still picture the shock and fear etched on the faces of my crew members. The soldiers, reserved for a war zone, approached them and demanded the keys to their equipment, but alas, the keys were in the possession of another team member, who was not present at that moment. Without hesitation, they instructed the technicians to break their locks. When the crew finally arrived at the filming location, they were visibly shaken. I could sense the tension in the air, the excitement of shooting a film overshadowed by the harsh reality they had just faced. Recognizing that they were in no fit state to create art under such duress, I made the difficult decision to call off the day's shoot.

Parthajit Baruah: How do you write stories for your films?

Aribam Syam Sharma: I don't write stories myself. Instead, I often take stories from M.K. Binodini, with whom I have collaborated on several films, including *Olangthagee Wangmadasoo* (1979), *Imagi Ningthem* (1981),

Paokhum Ama (1984), and *Ishanou* (1990). After we decide on a story, I work closely with the writer to develop the script and scenario, which can be a time-consuming process. As we work together, changes and adjustments are made. I don't just take a story from a writer and then work on it independently. Rather, I sit down with the writer and discuss the subject matter in detail, and we collaborate on the script writing process. This is the approach I've taken for all of my films.

Parthajit Baruah: When you're shooting, do you improvise your script during the shooting process?

Aribam Syam Sharma: Yes, I do, and it also depends on the location. In a studio, you can organize everything precisely according to your plan. For example, if you're making a room for a scene, you'll have a detailed drawing. However, when I'm shooting on location, especially if the location particularly inspires me, there's no set, no studio. I haven't worked in a studio for my films; I have to adapt to the location. Of course, the script provides the foundation. But the location rarely matches precisely what you envision for a specific scene. It's simply not possible. Therefore, I make adjustments, though not major ones. I adapt the shots to best suit the location.

Parthajit Baruah: In your film, did you intentionally subvert the stereotypical portrayal of a stepmother?

Aribam Syam Sharma: Yes, the film's story itself challenges that stereotype. It's based on a true story—a story that M.K. Binodini drew from the life of her neighbour. This element of realism resonated strongly, particularly in America. Audiences there found it hard to believe that such a situation could happen in real life.

Parthajit Baruah: What is your perspective on women, as reflected in your films?

Aribam Syam Sharma: You'll notice in my films that I don't portray "bad" characters as inherently evil. I believe humans aren't inherently bad; rather, it is their circumstances that shape their actions, affecting both men and women. There's no clear-cut dichotomy of "black and white" morality; life is full of grey areas. This contrasts with commercial films, where villains are often depicted as purely evil. To me, that's an outdated concept. We share the Shantiniketan philosophy that people are not born inherently evil. We believe that circumstances mould them, for better or worse. So, in my films, women are portrayed as human beings, often possessing considerable strength. We believe that in Manipur, in particular, women are not treated the same way, like other parts of India.

Parthajit Baruah: Could you share your impressions of the screening of *Imgi Ningthem* at the Indian Panorama?

Aribam Syam Sharma: Unfortunately, I couldn't attend the screening myself, but M.K. Binodini, Y. Roma, R. K. Bidur, and K. Ibohal were there to represent the film. When it was screened at the Indian Panorama, the response was modest at best. It's understandable, though—who would be inclined to watch a film by an unfamiliar director featuring unknown actors from a small state like Manipur?

Parthajit Baruah: What are your views and experiences as a filmmaker regarding film festivals and regional recognition?

Aribam Syam Sharma: Being a filmmaker has been a wonderful experience for me. I have travelled to many film festivals both in India and abroad. I appreciate the focus on regional films in these festivals, especially for North-East India. However, I want to clarify something about the idea of "regional" in art. In my opinion, art should not be limited by labels like regional or national. This distinction seems to come from the Indian government's current structure. For example, the Sangeet Natak Academy refers to works in different languages as "regional languages."

When it comes to National Awards, I have a problem with how films are categorized. For instance, if a Manipuri film wins a National Award, it's often labelled as a regional film as well. To me, this makes it seem like a "B" category award. I have protested this classification because I believe if it's recognized at the national level, it shouldn't be considered just regional.

Parthajit Baruah: Why do you think regional languages are important in films and art?

Aribam Syam Sharma: I think regional languages are very important in films and art. Every language has its own culture, feelings, and special characteristics.

When we create art, it should show who we are and our own experiences, which is best done in our own language. This honesty connects well with audiences and helps keep our cultural heritage alive and diverse. While languages like Hindi can help us communicate. It is also a regional language. Only in exchange of ideas, Hindi is used as lingua franca. It is good, let it be there.

Parthajit Baruah: Did you face any discrimination when you first went to Bombay because you are from the North-East, specifically Manipur?

Aribam Syam Sharma: Yes, I did. They didn't know where Manipur was, and that was a bit of a challenge. But I didn't let it bother me. We North-Easterners often face this problem when we go to other parts of India. People don't know much about our region and sometimes that leads to misunderstandings and discrimination.

Parthajit Baruah: Why do you think the northeast is often misunderstood or seen differently by people in other parts of India, sir?

Aribam Syam Sharma: I'm not saying this to criticize any particular group, but to highlight a reality. There are differences in features among Indians - the Aryans, the South Indians, and the people from the northeast have their own distinct features, which are Mongoloid. It's a fact that we can't ignore. Even when I travelled to Singapore for a film festival, my Indian passport didn't seem convincing to the security officer, who thought I didn't look like a typical Indian. He associated Indians with beards and long kurtas. It's situations like these that show how little people know about the northeast and its people.

Parthajit Baruah: What do you think about the representation of North-Eastern artists in Bollywood films?

Aribam Syam Sharma: It's a very important topic. I believe our features are beautiful, and we should be proud of them. Unfortunately, many people do not recognize North-Eastern artists as Indian. For example, when Priyanka Chopra was chosen to play Mary Kom, they picked her because she is a well-known Bollywood face, not because she looked like Mary Kom. This shows that a lot of people in India do not accept the faces of North-Easterners. When films like *Milkha Singh* are made, I don't think our local artists get the chance to play such roles. This is a reality we need to address.

Parthajit Baruah: What are your thoughts on how authorities treat filmmakers from the North-East?

Aribam Syam Sharma: I often see that authorities treat North-Eastern filmmakers unfairly. For instance, at the Indian Panorama, my film *Sanabi* was featured the same year as Shekhar Kapur's film *Phoolan Devi.* Kapur got to speak with the press for as long as he wanted, while directors like Dr. Bhabendranath Saikia, Jahnu Barua, and I only had half an hour for our press conference. Finally, we chose to walk out.

Parthajit Baruah: What is your perspective on the current condition of Manipuri cinema and the direction it is heading?

Aribam Syam Sharma: Right now, we are seeing a rise in the number of digital films being made. While this is positive, it comes with the need for proper training and guidance. It's essential for filmmakers to be sincere in their storytelling and to reflect their genuine experiences and the changes in our society. In traditional filmmaking, we were meticulous with our shots, but I find that many digital filmmakers today do not exercise the same care. Training is crucial; young filmmakers should come into the industry with a solid foundation. When I worked as an assistant director for *Matamgi Manipuri*, I gained a deep understanding of the filmmaking process.

Unfortunately, many of the new generation of filmmakers are not being true to themselves. Authenticity is key in creativity. If you want to create something meaningful, it has to come from an original place; you shouldn't merely imitate others.

Parthajit Baruah: What is your advice to the young generation of filmmakers?

Aribam Syam Sharma: My primary advice is to be true to themselves. Many young filmmakers struggle with this. You must be true to yourself to make original work. Don't fall into the trap of imitation. Your approach, your vision – everything should spring from your own unique perspective.

Remember, filmmaking offers a vast array of choices in terms of shots and angles. Ultimately, the director is the one making those decisions, not the cameraman. The director guides the cameraman to take the desired shots. So, don't compromise your artistic vision. Avoid cheating yourself by simply copying others. You can certainly learn from established filmmakers, but always remain true to your own voice. And remember, mastering the technical aspects of filmmaking, including its grammar, is essential. Filmmaking is a journey of self-discovery. You must have unwavering faith in your abilities and trust your instincts. Above all, resist the urge to imitate.

Filmography

Pabung Aribam has directed a remarkable 15 feature films and 31 non-feature films, in addition to composing music for 25 films. His work has earned him a total of 15 National Awards, comprising six for feature films and nine for non-feature films.

LAMJA PARSURAM

Year of Release: 1974

Format: 35 mm Black & White

Running time: 139 minutes'

Producer: G. Narayan Sharma (N.S. Films)

Direction & Music: Aribam Syam Sharma

Story: Gitchandra Tongbra

Screenplay: Elangbam Dinamani Singh

Cinematography: Sankar Banerjee

Editor: Madhusudan Banerjee

Language: Meitei/Manipuri

Playback Singers: Aribam Syam Sharma, Khun Joykumar, Kshetrimayum Rashi, Chongtham Kamala

Cast: Kangabam Tomba, Wahengbam Bedamani, G. Narayan Sharma, Yengkhom Roma, Huirem Manglem, Kshetrimayum Rashi, Gurumayum

Jayantakumar

Recognition: The film had a remarkable run of over 100 days, establishing itself as the first hit feature film in Manipuri cinema.

SHAPHABEE

Year of Release: 1976

Format: 35 mm Black & White

Running time: 116 minutes

Producer: G. Narayan Sharma (N.S. Films, Imphal)

Direction & Music: Aribam Syam Sharma

Story & Screenplay: Sarangthem Bormani

Cinematography: Deojibhai Padhiar

Editor: Madhusudan Banerjee

Lyrics: Konsaba Ibochou. G. Joykumar Sharma

Playback Singers: Jamuna, Khun Joy & Aheiljam Shyam

Language: Meitei/Manipuri

Cast: Subadani, Manbi, Rashi, Tomba, N.Tombi, Keshoram, Babu, Shanti, Gouri, Upen & others

Recognition: National Award for the Best Manipuri Film

OLANGTHAGEE WANGMADASOO

Year of Release: 1979

Format: 35 mm Black & White

Running time: 136 minutes

Producer: G. Narayan Sharma (N.S. Films, Imphal)

Direction: Aribam Syam Sharma

Story & Screenplay: M.K. Binodini Devi

Music Director: Aribam and Joy

Cinematography: Deojibhai Padhiar

Sound: Tomba Sharma

Language: Meitei/Manipuri

Cast: Tomba, Roma, Rashi, Keshoram, Tondon, Narmada, Meenakumari and Joy Kumar Sharma

Recognition: National Award for the Best Manipuri Film. It is the longest running film till date in the history of Manipuri Cinema.

IMAGI NINGTHEM

Year of Release: 1981

Format: 35 mm Black & White

Running time: 91 minutes

Producer: K. Ibohal Sharma (X - Cine, Imphal)

Director: Aribam Syam Sharma

Story & Screenplay: M.K. Binodini

Cinematography: K. Ibohal Sharma

Editor: Madhusudan Banerjee

Music Director: Khundrakpam Joykumar

Language: Meitei/Manipuri

Cast: Rashi, Jamini. Bhubaneshwari. Mangi, Manglem, Master Leikhendra & others. **Recognition:**

- Grand Prix at the Festival des 3 Continents, Nantes, France in 1982
- National Award for the Best Manipuri Film and also National Award for the Best Child Actor
- Indian Panorama, MOMA, New York & International Film Festivals across the globe which Includes-Festival des 3 Continents, Denver IFF, London FF, Locarno IFF, Montreal IFF, IFFI among others.

PAOKHUM AMA

Year of Release: 1984

Format: 16 mm colour

Running time: 54 minutes'

Producer: Film Division

Direction & Music: Aribam Syam Sharma

Story & Screenplay: M.K. Binodini

Cinematography: K. Ibohal and Daoji Sharma

Editor: Madhusudan Banerjee

Music: Khundrakpam Joykumar

Language: Meitei/Manipuri

Cast: Yengkhom Roma, Kangabam Tomba, Soraisam Dhiren, Huirem Manglem, Thokchom Ongbi Jamini, Kshetrimayum Rashi and others

Recognition: Tyneside Film Festival, UK

ISHANOU

Year of Release: 1991

Format: 35 mm Colour

Running time: 90 minutes

Producer: Aribam Syam Sharma for Doordarshan, Guwahati

Direction & Music: Aribam Syam Sharma

Story & Screenplay: M.K. Binodini

Cinematography: Girish Padhiar

Editor: Ujjal Nandy

Music: Aribam Syam Sharma

Language: Meitei/Manipuri

Cast: Anoubam Kiranmala, Kangabam Tomba, Baby Molly, Manbi, Soraisam Dhiren & others

Recognition:

A 'Selection Official' in the 44th Cannes Film Festival in 'Un Certain Regard'.

- Screened at various International Film Festivals across the globe which includes - London Film, Festival des 3 Continents, Singapore IFF, Hawaii IFF, Fribourg IFF, Vancouver IFF, Seattle IFF, Toronto IFF, IFFI among others.

- National Award for the Best Manipuri Film (Best Feature Film in Each of the Language Other Than Those Specified in the Schedule VIII of the Constitution)
- Special Mention for the Actor (female) in the National Film Festival Award for the Best Feature Film in the Manipur State Film Festival

SANABI

Year of Release: 1995

Format: 35 mm Colour

Running time: 88 minutes

Producer: National Film Development Corporation (NFDC) Ltd. & Doordarshan

Direction & Music: Aribam Syam Sharma

Story & Screenplay: M.K. Binodini

Cinematography: Sunny Joseph

Editor: Ujjal Nandy

Music: Aribam Syam Sharma

Language:Meitei/Manipuri

Cast: R.K. Sushila, Haorongbam Deben, Takhellambam Nabakumar, Heisnam Ongbi Indu, Thokchom Ongbi Jamini Lala, Y. Kumarjit& others

- **Recognition:**
- Won the Rajat Kamal for Best Regional Film in the National Film Festival in 1996
- Screened at the Cairo International Film Festival, Egypt, December, 1996
- Screened in the Indian Panorama section of the 27th IFFI at New Delhi in January, 1996

SHINGNABA

Year of Release: 1998

Format: 16mm Colour

Running time: -----

Producer: Films Division, Mumbai

Direction & Music: Aribam Syam Sharma

Story & Screenplay: Lamabam Birmani

Cinematography: Ph. Sharatchandra Sharma

Editor: Ujjal Nandy

Sound: Shantimo Sharmas

Language: Meitei/Manipuri

Cast: Makhonmani, Shashibala, Nabakumar, Jamini, Jiban & others.

PAARI

Year of Release: 2000

Format: 35mm Colour

Running time: 54 minutes

Producer: Children's Film Society, India

Direction & Music: Aribam Syam Sharma

Story & Screenplay: Aribam Gautam

Cinematography: Phurailatpam Imocha

Editor: Ujjal Nandy

Sound: Shantimo Sharma

Music: Ngagom Ebopishak

Language: Meitei/Manipuri

Cast: Master R.K. Surchandra, Master Telem Imotomba, Master G. Ashutosh, Master Jiban, Lourembam Keshworjit, and others

Recognition:

It was the first Children film in Manipuri Cinema. It was screened at the 12th International Children's Festival of India, Hyderabad, 2001. It was The film was screened at the National Children's Film Festival (NCFF) 2010 in Guwahati, at both the 2nd Children's Film Festival and the 4th Children's Film Festival in 2013 in Imphal.

ASHANGBA NONGJABI

Year of Production: 2003

Format: Betacam SP

Running time: 63 minutes

Producer: Aribam Syam Sharma

Direction & Music: Aribam Syam Sharma

Story & Screenplay: M.K. Binodini

Cinematography: Irom Maipak

Editor: Leichiklen

Playback Singer: Khundrakpam Joykumar

Language: Meitei/Manipuri

Cast: Bhogen, Khuraijam Lingjelthoibi, Ningthoujam Rina, Huirem Manglem, Kangabam Tomba& others

CROSSROADS

Year of Production: 2008

Format: Digital

Running time: 110 minutes

Producer: Aribam Syam Sharma

Director: Aribam Syam Sharma

Story & Screenplay: Aribam Syam Sharma

Cinematography: Irom Maipak

Editor: O. Gautam

Music Director: Aribam Uttam Sharma

Language: Meitei/Manipuri

Cast: Haraba, Karnajit, Sachidananda, Deepak & others

MIRAANG

Year of Production: 2011

Format: Digital

Running time: 84 minutes

Producer: Aribam Syam Sharma

Director: Aribam Syam Sharma

Story: Arambam Samarendra

Screenplay: Arambam ongbi Memchoubi

Music Director: Aribam Uttam Sharma

Cinematography: Irom Maipak

Editor: O. Gautam

Language: Meitei/Manipuri

Cast: Olen, Tonthoi, Reena, Sorojini, Lamyanba, Raj & Bijesh

LEIPAKLEI

Year of Release: 2012

Format: Digital Running time: 75 minutes

Producer: Aribam Syam Sharma

Director: Aribam Syam Sharma

Story: Arambam Samarendra

Screenplay: Arambam ongbi Memchoubi

Cinematography: Irom Maipak

Editor: Oinam Gautam Singh

Music Director: Aribam Uttam Sharma

Language: Meitei/Manipuri

Cast: Leishangthem Tonthoi, Lairenjam Olen, Gurumayum Kalpana, Thingom Pritam Baby Rainy & others

Recognition

- National Award for the Best Manipuri Film
- Screened at the Jeonju International Film Festival, Jeonju, South Korea Kolkata Film Festival
- Opening Film of the Gauhati International Film Festival.
- Habitat Film Festival, New Delhi

DASHA

Year of Release: 2013

Format: Digital

Running time: 76 minutes

Producer: Aribam Syam Sharma

Director: Aribam Syam Sharma

Story: Arambam Samarendra

Screenplay: Arambam ongbi Memchoubi

Music Director: Aribam Uttam Sharma

Cinematography: Irom Maipak

Editor: O. Gautam

Language: Meitei/Manipuri

Cast: Deekey, Ritu, Bijesh, Minakumari, Linjelthoibi & others

NONGPHADOK LAKPA ATITHI

Year of Production: 2019

Format: Digital

Running time: 74 minutes

Producer: Deepak Sarmah

Direction: Aribam Syam Sharma

Written: M. K. Binodini Devi & Lamabam Viramani

Screenplay: Aribam Syam Sharma

Story: Lamabam Viramani

Cinematography: Irom Maipak

Editor: Gurumayum Ashutosh

Music: Aribam Syam Sharma

Language: Meitei/Manipuri

Cast: Ningthoujam Rina, Lairenjam Olen, Kangabam Tomba, Redy Yumnam, Chingtham Sarmila and others.

Recognition: It was the opening film of the 12th International Guwahati Film Festival in 2020. It was also officially selected for the 5th North-East Film Festival in Pune, showcasing "Fragrances from the North-East."

Non-fiction

Here are the nine non-fiction films that won National Awards.

1. ***The Deer on the Lake*** **(1989):** National Film Award for Best Environment/Conservation/Preservation Film at the 37th National Film Awards.
2. ***Indigenous Games of Manipur*** **(1990):** National Film Award for Best Exploration/Adventure Film at the 38th National Film Awards.
3. ***Meitei Pung*** **(1991):** Special Mention Award at the 39th National Film Awards.
4. ***Orchids of Manipur*** **(1993):** Best Environment/Conservation/Preservation Film at the 41st National Film Awards. Screened at the Yamagata International Documentary Film Festival 2019, Japan. Participated in International Wildlife Film Festival, Morocco, 1994.
5. ***Yelhou Jagoi*** **(1995):** National Film Award for Best Anthropological/Ethnographic Film at the 43rd National Film Awards. Screened at the Yamagata International Documentary Film Festival 2019, Japan.
6. ***Thang-Ta: The Martial Art of Manipur (1999):*** National Film Award for Best Arts/Cultural Film at the 47th National Film Awards.

7. ***The Monpas of Arunachal Pradesh* (2001):** Best Anthropological/Ethnographic Film at the 49th National Film Awards.

8. ***Guru Laimayum Thambalngoubi Devi* (2005):** National Film Award for Best Biographical Film at the 54th National Film Awards.

9. ***Manipuri Pony* (2012):** National Film Award for Best Exploration/Adventure Film (Including sports) at the 60th National Film Awards.

Acknowledgements

My first meeting with Pabung Aribam in Itanagar, Arunachal Pradesh, in 2016 was the catalyst for this book. From that point, I engrossed myself in the study of his films. This book represents the result of that effort, enriched by the invaluable support of many. Without their support and generosity, this project would not have been possible.

First and foremost, I would like to express my profound gratitude to Aribam Syam Sharma sir for allowing me to write a book on his films. His belief in my vision has always driven me to push boundaries and strive for excellence. I am deeply appreciative of his sharing foreground and background of his films. I would like to express my sincere gratitude to Dr Aribam Uttam Sharma for his invaluable insights following his review of the first draft of my book. His feedback has played a significant role in shaping the final version. I extend my heartfelt thanks to Dhruva Aribam, whose support has been a constant source of encouragement throughout this journey and allowing me to use the film stills and workings. I would also like to express my sincere gratefulness to Gurumayum Ashutosh for providing access to some of Pabung's films, film stills and working stills in 2016. His willingness to share these resources has been instrumental in the research and development of this book. I found Pabung's autobiography, Living Shadows (published in 2006 by the Gauhati Cine Club in Guwahati, Assam), incredibly helpful. When I was reviewing the films he mentioned in the interview, I was able to quickly cross-checking them in his book. I'm deeply grateful for this resource, and I commend the Gauhati Cine Club for publishing such a valuable book.

A special note of thanks goes to Arti Karkhanis ma'am. Her support in allowing me to watch Pabung Aribam's films and access the library of the National Film Archive of India (NFAI) has been crucial to the completion of this work. The resources available at NFAI enriched my research and provided me with a deeper understanding of his films.

I am also grateful to my friends: Pradip Kurbah of Meghalaya, Kivini Shohe of Nagaland, Utpal Borpujari and Bitopan Borborah of Assam, Haobam Paban Kuman and Bobby Wahengbam of Manipur, for their insightful comments. I am grateful to filmmaker Akanshya Bhagabati. I am deeply indebted to filmmakers Suraj Dowerah, Monjul Baruah, and Khanjan Kishor Nath for their consistent support during this writing process.

Lastly, I would like to dedicate this book to all aspiring filmmakers and scholars eager to explore the rich storytelling of Aribam Syam Sharma. I believe this book will open new avenues for academics, cinephiles, and researchers alike.

I am deeply indebted to Ukiyoto Publishing House for recognizing the immense value of legendary filmmakers like Pabung Aribam and for taking the initiative to publish a book dedicated to his remarkable legacy. My heartfelt gratitude goes to every member of the Ukiyoto team for their patience and unwavering support throughout this journey.

Bibliography

1. Bidur, R. K. (2021). *A glimpse into the Manipuri cinema* (50 years of Manipuri cinema: Stories we breathe). Manipur State Film Development Society.

2. Bobby Wahengbam. (2018). *Matamgi Manipur - The first Manipuri feature film.* Angomningthou Preservation and Documentation.

3. Bordwell, D. *On the history of film style.* Harvard University Press.

4. Chabria, S. (n.d.). Introduction. In *100 years of cinema: A festival of films, celebrating one hundred years of cinema.* National Film Archive of India, Manipur State Film Development Society, & North Eastern Zonal Cultural Centre.

5. Hluna, J. V. (2013). *History and ethnic identity formation in North-East India.* Concept Publishing Company Pvt. Ltd.

6. Kongbam, M. (2021). *Manipuri cinema.* In Ningthoukhongjam, R. D., & Wangkhei, N. P. (Eds.). Imphal, Manipur: First edition.

7. Kongbam, M. (2021). *A glimpse of Manipuri cinema* (50 years of Manipuri cinema: Stories we breathe). Manipur State Film Development Society.

8. Kumar, B. B. (2007). *Problems of ethnicity in North-East India.* Concept Publishing Company Pvt. Ltd.

9. Rajadhyaksha, A., & Willemen, P. *Encyclopaedia of Indian cinema*. Routledge Taylor & Francis Group.

10. Rajesh, S. (1997). *A report on the seminar & symposium on Manipuri cinema* (25 years of Manipuri cinema, 1972-1997, Souvenir). Manipur State Film Development Society.

11. Sarin, V. I. K. *India's north-east in flames*. Vikas Publishing House Pvt Ltd.

12. Sharma, A. S. (2006). *Living shadows*. Gauhati Cine Club. Guwahati, Assam.

13. Singh, L. C. (2021). In his message (25 years of Manipuri cinema, 1972-1997).

14. Verma, R. (2013; 2017). *History of North East India* (Second ed.). Mittal Publication.

Photographs

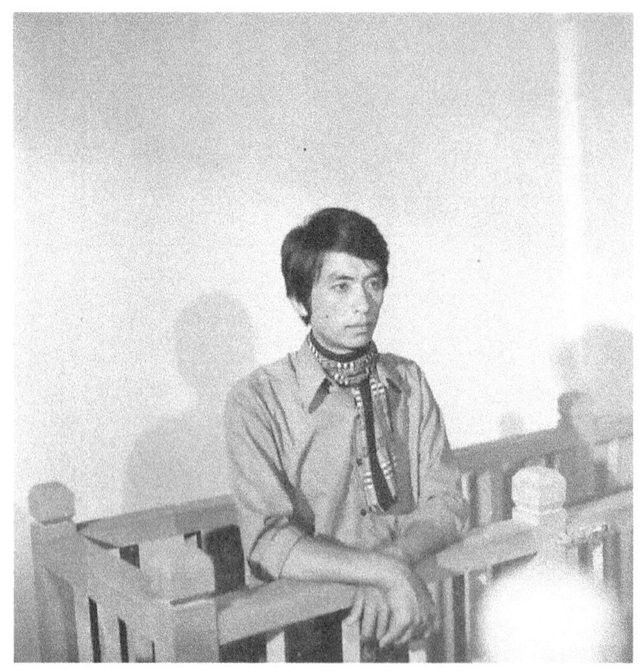

Figure 1. Tomba in *Lamja Parshuram*.

Image copyright: Aribam Syam Sharma Archive

Figure 2. G. Narayan Sharma in *Lamja Parshuram*

Image copyright: Aribam Syam Sharma Archive

Figure 3. Aribam Syam Sharma on the set of *Shaphabee*
Image copyright: Aribam Syam Sharma Archive

Figure 4. Film still of *Shaphabee*

Image copyright: Aribam Syam Sharma Archive

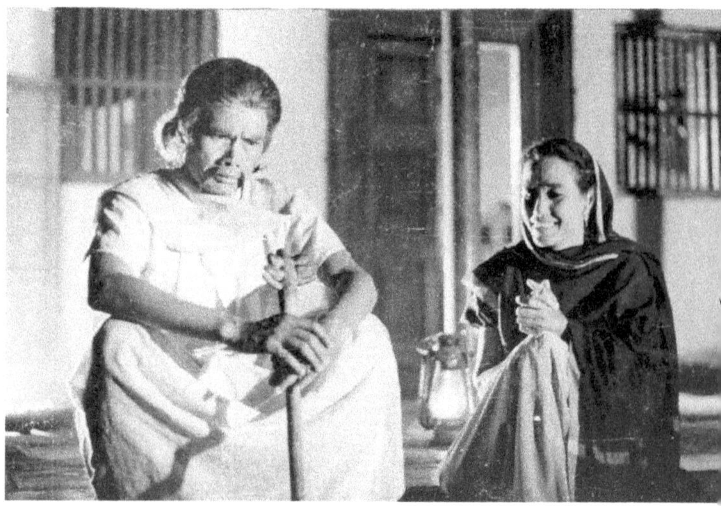

Figure 5. Film still of *Olangthagee Wangmadasoo*

Image Copyright: Aribam Syam Sharma Archive

Figure 6. Aribam Syam Sharma on the set of *Olangthagee Wangmadasoo*

Figure 7. Master Leikhen in *Imagi Ningthem*

Image Copyright: Aribam Syam Sharma Archive

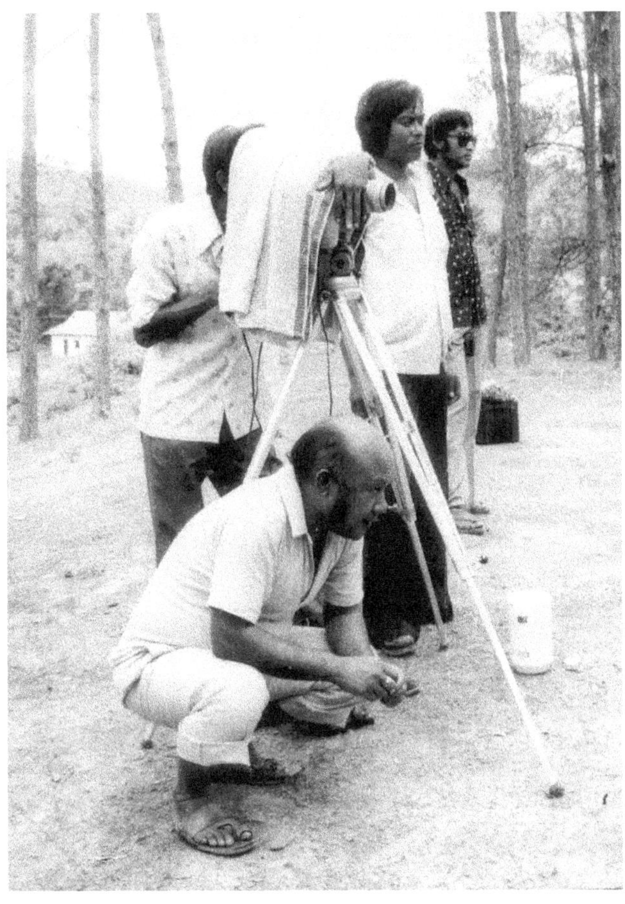

Figure 8. Aribam Syam Sharma on the set of *Imagi Ningthem*

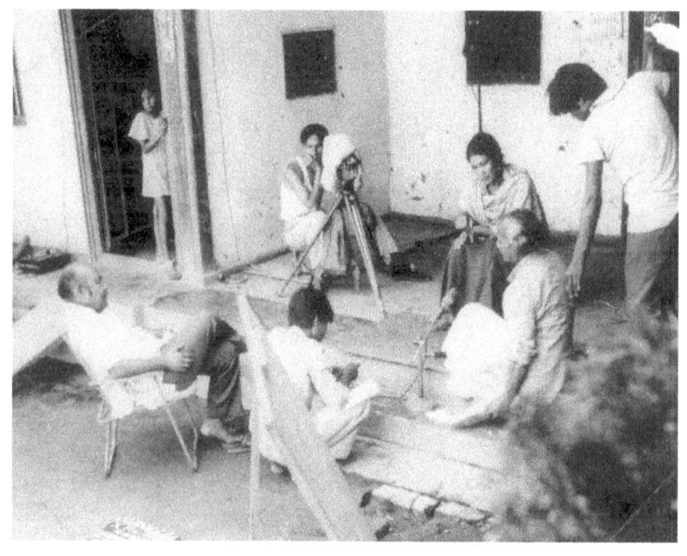

Figure 9. Aribam Syam Sharma on the set of *Imagi Ningthem*

Image Copyright: Aribam Syam Sharma Archive

Figure 10. Aribam Syam Sharma on the set of *Imagi Ningthem*

Image Copyright: Aribam Syam Sharma Archive

Figure 11. Aribam Syam Sharma during a scene of *Lai Haraoba*

Figure 12. Kiranmala in *Ishanou*

Image Copyright: Aribam Syam Sharma Archive

Figure 13. Tomba with Kiranma in *Ishanou*
Image Copyright: Aribam Syam Sharma Archive

Figure 14. Film still of *Marams*

Image Copyright: Aribam Syam Sharma Archive

Figure 15. Aribam Syam Sharma rehearsing songs for *Matamgi Manipur* at Imphal

Image Copyright: Aribam Syam Sharma Archive

Figure 16. Aribam Syam Sharma as Tonsna, (Ibohal's father) with Indira and Roma in *Matamgi Manipur* (1972)

Figure 17. From the left Napo RZ Thanga, Aribam Syam Sharma sir, Meena Longjam, Tribeny Rai

and Kivini Shohe at the Itanagar Film Festival, 2016

Image Copyright: Parthajit Baruah

Figure 18 Author with Aribam Syam Sharma sir and his wife, Gurumayum Radhapyari Devi, 2016

Figure 19. Aribam Syam Sharma, Monjul Baruah and the author

Figure 20. During the interview with the lead actress, Leishangthem Tonthoi of the film *Leipaklei* (2012)

Figure 21. Aribam Syam Sharma with his film Ishanou at the Cannes Film Festival

Image Copyright: Aribam Syam Sharma Archive

Figure 22. Aribam Syam Sharma with his film *Imagi Ningthem* at Nantes, France

Image Copyright: Aribam Syam Sharma Archive

Figure 23. Scriptwriter MK Binodini

Image Copyright: Aribam Syam Sharma Archive

Figure 24. Film poster, *Sanabi* (1995)

Image Copyright: Aribam Syam Sharma Archive

About the Author

Parthajit Baruah is an Indian film historian and filmmaker. He completed his postgraduate studies in English literature at Fergusson College, Pune University, followed by an M.Phil. on *Film Adaptation: Shakespeare on Celluloid* and a Ph.D. on *Literature and Film: Shakespeare in Indian Cinema in the select Indian films*. He has authored several books on film, including *Face to Face: The Cinema of Adoor Gopalakrishnan* (HarperCollins, 2016), *A History of India's North-East Cinema: Deconstructing the Stereotypes* (Bloomsbury Academic, 2024), and *Jyotiprasad, Joymoti, Indramalati and Beyond: History of Assamese Cinema* (Krantikal Prakashan, 2021), He did two research projects on films at the National Film Archive of India (NFAI) in Pune. He has presented research papers on film at various institutions, including Queen's University, London, MAHE in Dubai, and Edinburgh University in Scotland. Baruah has directed 13 documentaries and one feature film, *The Nellie Story* (2023). He received the Assam State Film Critic Award from the Government of Assam and the Prag Channel Film Critic Award.